THE

THIRD

RETURN

THE

THIRD

RETURN

MONICA M. MEDINA

Indigo River Publishing

Indigo River Publishing
3 West Garden Street, Ste. 718
Pensacola, FL 32502
www.indigoriverpublishing.com

The Third Return | Monica Medina
ISBN: 978-1-950906-68-0 (paperback)
LCCN: 2021906458

Edited by Earl Tillinghast
Interior design by Robin Vuchnich
Cover Design by Evie Shaffer, visual artist

To those who have lost their voice and fallen to senseless evil;
my hope is that you will find the beauty, happiness and
freedom again
which life has been trying to offer you.
TAKE IT BACK
for the next flourishing steps of your life and for the
little eyes around the corner.

To my brothers; I'm lucky to have you then, to have you now
and
to have you always.
Our bond is relentless.

To Mom, for your never-failing protection and lasting love.
I will never be able to repay you.
This is for you.

Love,
Your daughter.

Contents

Introduction

"It always seems impossible until it's done."
—Nelson Mandela

SOPHOMORE YEAR OF HIGH SCHOOL, a dormant part of me was awakened after reading the novel *The Breakable Vow* by Kathryn Ann Clark in my literature class. I remember how concerned I felt being able to relate to a book like that. The fear shouting from those pages felt all too similar to the last 10 years of my life. During class, I sat at my desk, listening to students read aloud what I had read the night before and wondered if others were thinking what I was: *Is this happening to anyone else?* If you haven't read it, it's a great first eye opener to the subject of domestic violence. Why does she stay? Why doesn't she just leave? So many questions raced through my mind as I read through the book. At the time, I would never have guessed that my own experiences would eventually answer all those questions.

I felt as if a part of my mind was unlocked. How relieved I felt to have found answers that finally gave the chaos in my day-to-day life a startling clarity. It was as if someone was removing cobwebs from a corner of my brain that had long been dark and dormant.

In short, this novel displays domestic violence and the many ways a woman may try to leave, along with the murky bucket of emotional pain, struggle, uncertainty, self-doubt and relapse that often closely accompanies these relationships.

These romances aren't wearing flashing warning signs nor do they have bright orange *Caution Ahead* posts mounted miles before the rough patch. No. They start like most intriguing, romantic, love-struck stories. Yet, somewhere along the butterfly trail with yellow sunshine faces singing and trees blossoming it turns into a fast, downward spiral on a dangerous path where the emotional exchange quickly and sadly becomes toxic and futile. Like many provocative and attention-grabbing topics, domestic violence is very easy to judge from the outside looking in, so I urge you to read just a little further before casting judgment.

Perhaps you've come to this book and it's the first time you're opening your heart and mind to this world. Or maybe, you've devoted twenty to thirty years of your life to a man or woman who has stripped you of all your self-worth, respect and motivation for life—or so you have come to believe. Regardless of the path that has led you here, my heart is happy to know this book has found its way to your hands.

For those of you coming from violence, how did you make it here? Not here as in to this page or to this bookstore, library or wherever you stand or sit, but here to this point in your life? Does it look anything remotely close to this:

You've tried leaving. It didn't work. Maybe it even became

worse when you returned. At all hours, your mind races with fear and it seems like relief can't be found in anything or any place. You've given up the games and accepted this must be your fate. This is your punishment, you believe, for some inexplicable reason you deserve to be hurt and screamed at. Sleep has stopped bringing peace. Your friends and family helped you in the beginning, but even they have accepted this is how it is now. This is how you are. This how he is. This is how you are *together*. They've stopped trying; stopped coming around; stopped attempting to convince you that you deserve better because you just won't do better for yourself. They turn a blind eye. Keep their distance. It's too much on them to be involved. Maybe they call at late hours when he's not around, visit you at work because that's the only time they can see you and the only time you've allowed them to. Any gift or money you're expecting is sent to your PO Box instead of to your door. Maybe you don't work and that's not by choice, but by force. No access to money because he's convinced you, that you're incapable of working. Yet somehow, he still shames you for stressing him out with all the bills. He hurts you. Bad. Your children pretend to sleep but talk to you about the nights in the morning. As they speak, you cling to your sunglasses just trying to hide what you sense they already know.

Does this sound familiar? Had you always wanted your life this way? As a child, is this how you dreamt it to be? Of course not. Ask yourself what brought you to this life and how have you been living it for so long? If you're not happy with your answers, don't worry. We're about to change them.

The first question many people have when probing into the issues of domestic violence is *"Why doesn't she just leave?"*

Well guess what? Almost always, the victim and children involved are thinking the same thing. So, what's the problem? I was asking the same confusing question most people do when they discuss abusive relationships...

Why did she stay? Why did she return?

This question seems to boggle the minds of psychologists, therapists and mental health professionals everywhere as well as the family, the children and every relative involved. From my experience, this is what I have concluded.

Women *stay in abusive relationships* for the following reasons:

- **Fear & Control**: maintaining the abuser is often times the only sense of control the victim believes they have. The abuser provides this illusion of control. You are never *really* in control of what happens next, but the illusion works to his advantage and will keep you in the relationship longer. This is often why women *hope* the abuser is able to change. Because he has allowed you to believe that you somehow have control of his emotions and possess the power to change him. You don't.
- **Habit & Pattern**: Both individuals have developed a strong habit, a pattern neither one knows how to break. Since neither one is able to change it, the pattern continues to cycle and strengthen until change is introduced. Whatever change is introduced needs

to be done carefully and handled by a professional. This can be the most dangerous part but is a vital step towards breaking the cycle.

- **Love & Self:** The most important, I believe, is that women have somehow misconstrued the definition of Love. They have associated Love with Pain, Love with Forgiveness, Love with Fear, Love with something other than authentic Love. Reevaluating your definition of Love in every aspect of your life (with your partner, with your parents, with your children) is certain to bring some new insight.

Women *return to abusive relationships* for the following reasons:

- **Comfort in the Familiar:** The abuse is hard, but the unfamiliar can appear harder. Leaving the abuser seemed to be the right choice, but because he has stripped you of your confidence, independence and ability to love yourself, you automatically question if you're capable of living without him. This is planned and plays to what the abuser intended. Seek therapy to reestablish self-love, independence and confidence to embark on the unfamiliar.

- **Withdrawal:** After leaving, many women have said they miss their abuser. Or stranger, they miss the abuse itself. They don't know why. They don't understand it, but you're not crazy if you have, promise. Find strong support to keep you from relapsing. Change takes time to settle and often times women return too quickly, not allowing the full process of change to take place. Don't get in your own way. Be patient.

- **Hope:** Leaving allows the dust to settle and chaos to disperse. This is when the idea of Hope returns and seems to erase much of the horrible feelings you just had. This is a trap. Watch yourself. This is your chance to leave the cycle and change your entire life! You're most likely just moving towards what you believe is going to make you happy and at the moment, it seems to be him. It's not. Instead, fill your time with anything else that *really does* make you happy. The things you forgot about and haven't done in so long. The dancing, girls' night out, walks in the park or movie-nights-for-one that used to make you smile. Spend your money on YOU for once. If you have children, go out with them. Plan something to look forward to and do it! They most likely want to see more of you anyway, so get your abuser out of the spotlight of your life. Bring YOUR happiness back into YOUR life. Find yourself again and you'll forget all about…. what was his name?

In the personal pages ahead about my mother's battle with violence, she did just that. She found herself, she chose herself and she left. However, it's always easier to give advice than it is to take it, especially from someone who may not be professionally equipped to handle such dangerous territory. Friends and family may in fact have the right answers and the right heart, but there will always be obstacles to occur that only those with experience would anticipate. Find those professionals to help you leave.

Maybe you're at a point where your abuser has so much power over your heart and mind that you wonder what decisions you're capable of making. Over time through his spiteful control, cowardly violence and aggressive manipulation, your brightness has dulled. Now, what needs to be realized is that he can never take away your strength nor the beauty of your true essence to begin with. No one can.

Nonetheless, you may still have come to believe that you have no choices left to make. In truth, there may not be many, but there are still some and they are powerful ones at that! Ironically, what remains is all you really need in order to make a change for yourself, for your children, for your life. Your strength is there, within reach at this very moment, just waiting for you to use it and make a divine transformation. But will you?

Through my personal experience, I've seen how the decision to get out and the mindset of *I'm done, I've had enough* can be all the throttle you need to climb out of this. Your worst crutch is your own denial. There is no easy solution, and the risks are great. But there is a tremendous reward for overcoming this, just as many have seen before you.

For as long as I've been able to convert short term memories into long term memories, I have been a witness to the kind of screaming, yelling and beating that's commonly found in a hostile home. It is not something that is conjured up overnight, but rather is a long forming habit created through continuous cycles of behavior. Will you find the strength to break this wretched ritual: the one that has so spitefully and mischievously tricked you into believing *this is my fate, there's nothing I can do, I've tried, it doesn't work?* Well, karate chop that negativity in the jugular. You have to believe within the depths of your soul that a life of freedom does exist for yourself and for those little eyes around the corner. If you don't, your hopes will continue to seem like a mere mirage.

Speaking of those little eyes around the corner, maybe they're not so little anymore. Perhaps they're an individual on their way through adolescence just trying to figure themselves out and where they fit in the animal kingdom world of high school. Or they've managed to plunge through all that, figure it out as best they could, and are now writing the frightening horror story that is adulthood. I've certainly been there and remain there on some rare days. Growing up with the sound of my mother crying in the next room, watching her run for her life, and listening to him call her every horrid name has hindered every part of my life.

If you're the child who has witnessed or is witnessing violence, you've probably begun to notice its effect on you. If you're like many, you've always known there was something different in you, but didn't have the words to describe it until later on in life. Maybe it still doesn't make sense.

Throughout this book, I will be blatantly honest and forthcoming with you about the defeating transitions I was faced with because of my mother's choice to love an evil man. You'll see where I struggled in the balance of love and hate, acceptance and resentment, and compassion and rebellion. I was always haunted with feelings of incredible guilt when making decisions I knew in my heart were the right ones.

The experiences that came with my stepfather have taught me valuable lessons that will forever push me to be the person I want to be and leave behind the one I was with him. The ugly tradition of violence will no longer continue in my family's cycle, but it has come at no easy cost. I have had to differentiate and decide between the lessons that were truly helpful and the lessons that weren't lessons, but false and detrimental, emotional traps.

My mother is my life's inspiration and I've written this book with the leaping hope that her story can help you in yours. She is my life's motivation, the fire in my desire, and the everything of my heart. Honest. Her strength was stunning and admirable in more ways than can be counted and her journey has enlightened a thriving passion in me to choose a life led by love, not fear. Although I cherish her memory and share an everlasting connection as her daughter, there still remain differences between us; differences that can debilitate me if I allow them to.

Without a doubt, I am choosing to embrace life: one I am happiest with; one which no longer consists of the toxic emotional chaos that once consumed it. I choose now not only to live, but to happily thrive.

Even in her passing she has continued to teach me priceless values, some of which I could only have learned in her absence. Both her story and my own are the ones I would like to share with you now, so that you may find the beauty, peace and freedom again which life has been trying to offer you.

Take it back.

If you've been able to read on thus far and find your thumb is ready to turn the page, then maybe you feel like there is something here you can use. Go on. You've got this.

Mozart

June 8, 1995

SOUTH SIDE CHICAGO'S dreary brick homes and stone stoops were just about the best spot to be. Rough neighborhoods that turned into worse neighborhoods and alleys lit with a single orange street lamp flickering in the late hours of the night always made you consider taking a different path; South Mozart was the first street of my life to be called *home*. Most think of the ever-talented Wolfgang Amadeus Mozart who composed the famous classical piano pieces. Though I wish his melodies were what come to my mind, I have other, less pleasant, associations.

As a sophisticated three-year old, I sat in a hospital room with my mother who was laid on the bed and my stepfather who paced beside her while rationing out M&M's to me in my paper cup. I didn't understand what we were waiting for, but I didn't care since I was happily content with my candy.

Days later, I was sitting on my mother's bed as she tried propping up this heavy, uncoordinated white skinned, blonde haired thing on my lap. Underneath its large, swishy diaper were my tiny legs being crushed.

"Hey, look over here!" Mom snapped her fingers, holding something large and black that tried to capture our attention. *I'd seen this before; you're supposed to smile when she says smile. So why wasn't this thing listening?* As she spoke, the thing on my lap started coming alive creating all sorts of ridiculous, incoherent sounds.

I looked around Mom's bedroom and noticed new furniture. *That tall bed over there looks comfy. Why does this loud thing get to sleep in here with Mom and I have to sleep in a different room?* With unquenchable curiosity, I climbed up the tall blue crib. *Wow, this bed is way softer than mine.* It was decorated in the most comfortable green and white silky sheets I had ever felt. But just as I was on the verge of a peaceful sleep, Mom would always interrupt my drooping eyelids.

"Hey! Out of there!" her voice rang, "Get down!"

As I came to discover, that thing was a baby and he was fed warm bottles of milk while being rocked to sleep every night and then he was gently placed in his cloud-like crib. All of it was nothing I felt a part of until he began walking and talking. When he got a hold of these skills, we would wake up before anyone else and spend our weekend mornings watching cartoons. If we became bored, we played quietly upstairs with my Barbie dolls. If we became hungry, we poured ourselves bowls of cereal and crept up the stairs to my room, but usually our noise in the kitchen always woke someone up.

During the school weeks, I would be woken by a sleepy, slow moving man as he repeatedly tossed a pillow at my face. Ian was a tall, thin, light skinned man with Hispanic features. His dark, wrinkled eyes were nearly black at the pupil while his wispy coal hair surrounded a bald spot directly atop his head. His thin mustache always became smaller as his mouth tightened to release his angry words. When I gathered the strength to stir from my sleep, he would leave as if he had done his job.

I made my bed, carefully placing my stuffed animals in front of my pillows, and then dressed myself in the uniform which Mom had hung on my dresser the night before. My white tights, shiny black close-toed shoes, and flat white round-collared shirt under my blue plaid dress were my everyday uniform. I went straight downstairs into the bathroom to brush my teeth and wait for Ian to style my hair. He sat on the toilet seat cover, wetting the skinny comb in the sink and saturated my hair in water as he pulled through my tight curls. When he had my locks tightly slicked to a single spot, he'd tie it up, sometimes snapping his finger with the ball as he wrapped it around the bundle of hair. When it was tight, he gave me a push and sent me on my way.

Caleb and I sat at our plastic white, red and blue table eating cereal, eggs, waffles or whatever we were given for breakfast while watching reruns of Scooby Doo. Junior, my older brother by eight years from my mother's first marriage, would be waiting alone for his bus in the living room. Peering out the window, hanging over the couch, and covered in the long, draped curtains, he usually left unnoticed. Never did he say goodbye. Never did Ian make him breakfast.

When it was time to leave for school, we walked with Mom out the back door on a narrow sidewalk to the detached single car garage which was always entirely covered with lush green vines in the summer months. We drove out the alley in Mom's white SUV, embarking on the familiar ten-minute drive.

At our Baptist school, the only teachers in the church building were an elderly husband and wife. The students' work was independently self-taught via workbooks. The books had check points at which you had to ask for permission to "check" your work thus far against the score keys at the center podiums. I watched as the experienced kids wrote the answers down and went back to their seats where they filled in their blank work. It was a flawed system in more ways than one which I eventually learned caused irreparable damage to my early learning.

At the end of the school day, Mom picked up Caleb and me. We never had homework, so we always showered before dinner. We always argued who would go first, and when we finished, we would dress and sit down for dinner. It was pretty much an autopilot routine, but the constant arguments between Ian and Mom would often cause me to lose any appetite. He would scream at her from across the table or shout profanities from another room. Caleb and I usually sat quietly, waiting for him to stop. Many nights we would continue eating after he had left, and the house returned to silence. Other nights, when no end seemed to be in sight, Caleb and I eventually left the table unnoticed. If the arguing persisted, Mom escaped by getting us into bed and spending a lengthy amount of time at our side tucking us in.

At the end of the night when she sat by my side, she would remind me, "You know Papi doesn't mean that right? He's just being silly." She'd smile and grace my cheek with her soft embrace and goodnight kiss. To me, she was all definitions of beauty. A small woman with smooth glowing skin, shining hazel eyes, a gentle voice and a heart larger than her body could hold. Her strikingly large smile was caressed by prominent wrinkles that made her smile appear larger than it was. Her head of tight, winding curls lay thick around her neck, completing her sweet impression. She kissed me all over my face and hugged me tight enough to leave her scent with me for hours. As she left my room with the door open exactly to my liking, I knew she was only trying to prevent me from seeing Ian as he really was.

The way my Tia Carlita puts the story, Mom and Ian met on a blind date. Mom loved a man in uniform and Ian happened to be a Chicago police officer: a whole lot of uniform. He was a friend of the guy my Tia was dating at the time and it made sense to get them together. Well, they hit it off *so* well that Ian became my babysitter and not long after his babysitting days, Mom and I moved into his house on Mozart. When they married in 1995, that large blonde baby, Caleb, was born.

As Mom and Ian grew in their relationship, Mom legally divorced my biological father in 1996. At age 4, I went to court with them for a custody meeting. All the adults were asked to leave the room so I could be alone with a woman who asked me, "If you could have three wishes, what would they be?"

Who knows what I said for my first wish, but for my second and third request I responded with, "So that Rusty our dog will live forever and that mommy and daddy get back together." I don't remember having any bad feelings about their separation. It was just that I felt happier being with both of them together rather than apart. I was still getting to know Ian. He was nice to me, but he was still a stranger; one who didn't bring me the same comfort Mom and Dad brought me.

On the car ride home with Ian and Mom, she asked me, "So what did she say?" I sensed her curiosity.

15

"She asked me what my three wishes are," I responded nonchalantly, playing in the seat behind her.

"Oooh, okay." Leaning her ear over to hear me, she asked, "And what did you say?"

"I said I wish that Rusty would live forever and that you and daddy get back together." What I believed was light conversation turned into unsettling silence. I paused from my playing and looked up to see her mouth drop open and Ian piercing her with his stare. Mom instantly seemed worried and I sensed my response had caused it. *What did I say? Was that the wrong thing to say?* After a moment of prolonged silence, Mom carefully replied "Honey, Daddy and I are not getting back together." Feeling as if I was being punished, I sat in the backseat mute and still.

After their divorce was final, Dad had been appointed fifty percent custody with weekend visitation. So, when every Friday came I would reel with excitement. Mom would help me pack *way* too many outfits, and I would try to decide which of my favorite toys I wanted to take. She would dress me nicely and fix my hair in a ponytail slicked way too tight so as not to allow for a single strand of hair to straggle. Once in the car with Dad on the road to his house, I would ask, "Can I take it out?" He would always smile and reply with a, "Yeah, take it out."

There were many afternoons, however, when I didn't make it to Dad's car. Instead, I would sit eagerly in the living room, hanging my body over the couch and peering out the windows in search of his car. When I spotted Dad's ebony and gray van pulling up across the street, I rushed wildly to grab my things and head for the door, but I was stopped in my tracks. Mom and Ian went outside first, leaving me at the door. I dashed back to the window staring at them talk for what seemed like eternity. *What are they doing?*

I quickly learned that Ian's hostility towards my father usually meant I wasn't going anywhere. Instead of being in the car with my dad and listening to music while having our usual catch-up conversations, I watched the police arrive with flashing lights to diffuse the chaos Ian sparked. He always did something to ruin the day I had been looking forward to, anything to prevent me from leaving. I later learned that upon one of my father's arrivals, Ian slashed all four of the tires on his van, leaving my father and stepmother to have it towed back to their house and arranging another way back home. On that night, I didn't leave either.

Eventually, Dad started arranging my pick-ups at the police station since coming to the house was proving to be a dangerous and difficult task. And if Mom couldn't make it to the police station because Ian wouldn't allow her, Dad came to get me with his own police escort.

On the weekends when I managed to escape the house with Dad, I would return Sunday nights, feeling completely thrown off my routine. During the holiday season on a cold, snowy Sunday, I came back to see everyone putting up the Christmas tree in the living room. The snow swept in as Mom closed the door, and I saw boxes upon boxes of sparkling ornaments laid out on the couch just waiting to be hung. They were all so beautiful. All I wanted to do was hang them too, so I put my things upstairs in my room and rushed downstairs to join everyone, but made the mistake of happily greeting Ian with, "Daddy!"

Ian glared at me. "What did you call me?" No one spoke.

"Daddy?" I mumbled, not wanting the word to leave my mouth.

"Is that my name?" He turned to me and I shook my head.

"Is it?" he shouted, demanding I speak.

"No." I cautiously stepped away as he turned back around.

"Go to your room." He stood still, waiting for me to start walking.

Mom interjected, "Ian, it was just an accident. She didn't mean it."

"Did I ask you?" He shouted, slashing her sweet effort. And in that moment, I knew Mom could not help me, so there was no other option than to obey his order. As soon as I turned around, I was flooded with tears and walked slowly all the way back upstairs to my room; my sobbing had drenched my shirt by the time I made it to my bed.

My excitement had instantly been scorched away and replaced with fear. I cried alone in my room, eventually falling asleep. I learned very quickly that "Daddy" and "Papi" were not the same and although I didn't understand why, I couldn't let it happen again.

...

Junior and I didn't spend much time together. He eventually went back to live with my Dad because he and Ian never got along. When I was older he told me that one day he came home from school and Ian offered to help him with his homework. They sat at the formal oak dining table in the nice part of the house which was covered with a white lace cloth and dressed with crystal candle holders placed at the center. Having nearly no patience, Ian became increasingly agitated with teaching Junior. When his rage surpassed the point of reason, Ian grabbed the crystal candle holder and struck Junior across the head. For years, Junior had come to my bedside to tell me more of his made-up stories that made me laugh so hard. Instead of falling asleep, I would become wide awake, laughing at his nonsensical story about a pen and an eraser or the stick and the rock. As he rambled on, creating the story as he told it, I noticed the mark on his head and wondered how it got there. Never had I known that he experienced the same Ian I did.

...

I would make a mistake. I wouldn't listen or I would be much too rambunctious and wild when playing with Caleb. Whatever I did, it was usually small because I was 4 and only capable of so much. But there were times when I would get myself into "trouble" with Ian.

No one else was ever home when it happened, or at least no one made themselves known. Quite possibly so I would have no one to scream for. Sometimes I went first. Other times it was Caleb. Sometimes it was only Caleb. Sometimes it was only me.

When I heard my name calmly called from the master bedroom, I would come without hesitation—*that is, until I caught on.*

As soon as I stood in the doorway, I would see Ian standing there waiting for me with a cold, blank expression and a shiny black belt looped in his hand. I sank into myself; instantly wanting to disappear and immediately growing angry at myself for coming so willingly and not having allowed myself any chance of escape.

"Come here," he said sternly. My eyes began to fill with tears as he repeated himself, "Come here. Now."

His words ignited the fear within me. Sobbing uncontrollably, I said, "No."

"You're going to get it even worse if you don't come here now." He stood like a stone, unaffected. I took my time inching my way to the wall.

"Right now!" He sparked with impatience and I knew he meant every word. So I obeyed.

I faced the hideous, green colored wall, placed my hands on it, and watched my teardrops fall to the floor while he whipped me one unbearably painful time. The burn was enough to make the shaking of my body uncontrollable. Hysterical, I cried at the top of my lungs, the sting surging through my skin. I ran away to my room, locked the door, and watched the sunlight fade into darkness. My pillow became heavier and heavier.

For hours, I lay in my bed trying to catch my breath and tightly grasped my behind trying to rub the soreness away. But nothing helped. I lay in misery until I fell asleep. For the rest of the night, no one came to me, and the next day at school I sat in my seat with my rear still tender. This occurred more times than I can recall. When I would regain control of my tears and stop struggling to breathe, I would question if it really happened.

There was never any validation. Everyone always carried on normally and never mentioned it. Questions flooded my mind. *Why was this happening to me? Did anyone care that I was hurt? Did anyone care about me? Why didn't anyone help me?* After multiple nights of asking the same questions, I began to answer them myself.

Shy of 5 years old, I started to understand how to handle Ian. Everyone's silence told me no one wanted to get in his way and I quickly noticed how no one ever told him no. He was in charge. He told everyone what to do. He made the rules and I adapted.

I relied on instinct to avoid confrontation, to avoid getting into "trouble" and to avoid going back to that wall. I needed to follow his rules, never ask questions and always, always do what he said.

While treading Ian's dark waters, fear and uncertainty were controlling me: in my every move and in my every word. *Would this make him angry?* I had to wonder. I noticed everyone was dominated by the same fear. My pain would take a night to recover from, but it was always tolerable compared to what I'd hear and see Mom endure.

...

1995

I was barely attentive to the television in the living room as I sat with Omar, Ian's eighteen-year-old son from his first marriage. I focused on nothing other than the shouting down the hall. I could peer over the corner to see Ian standing over Mom and yelling into her face. Mom shoved him away, but Ian became enraged, only escalating with her every attempt to diffuse him. Every shout rang louder than the last, and I could feel the seed of fear growing wild.

I watched as Ian grabbed and pushed Mom against the wall. He held her tight, trapping her in his grasp. Holding a gun in his hand, he forced her into the bathroom. He slammed the door behind them and trapped her inside. I sat on the couch, staring at the bathroom door, wishing they hadn't disappeared from my sight. In terror, I cried alongside her cries. I was afraid of what was happening behind those doors, but even more terrified about what it would mean if they stopped.

Shocked, I sat there with Omar across from me. The TV was on silent. He stared at the glowing light and I watched as tears fell from his eyes.

"Ahhhhh! Omar! Ahhh, please! Please he-he-help me! Please!" Mom's pleas continued from the bathroom and shook the walls and bones in my body.

"Omar!" Ian shouted back, "Don't you come in here!" His tone ordered Omar to stay put. And Omar did.

Omar didn't move a single muscle from the sofa and Mom's shouts continued to shake the house.

I could barely speak over my weeping and choked breath, "Aren't you going to help her?" I was confused. "Why are we sitting here while she is screaming for help?"

"I … can't," Omar finally replied as his tears caught his words. He didn't bother to face me and deep, immense anger began to fill me. Complete helplessness smothered my thoughts, rearranging everything I knew. *Why? She needs you! She needs help! Why are we just sitting here?*

I mustered up the strength to speak again, "She needs you to help her." My lips trembled with panic as I sat clenching the couch pillows in agony as every moment passed without action.

He sniffled and wiped his cheek, "He said I can't."

"Omar! Pleeeease!" Mom's cries fell upon two powerless children. My heart continued to race. *Why are we just sitting here? Why are we just sitting here? Why are we just sitting here?* I was forced to swallow the appalling truth that Omar wasn't going to do anything. No one was going to do anything. Ian had made it so.

Hope was the only thing I had, and it proved a useless rescue.

The next morning, I was tremendously relieved to see Mom. I didn't know what the remainder of the night had brought her. I never asked.

We sat there. We just sat there. The thoughts still alarmed me. I was infuriated at my own helplessness, resentful of my own lack of ability and condemning Omar for not doing anything.

Still, to this day, I know many parents are tortuously asking their children to accept the same awful truth; *you are helpless.* Household dynamics continue to exist that are dominated by fear, not by love; by anger, not compassion; and by control, not guidance. For those children, there is no choice, because they have been raised to believe that they have none. *You can do nothing.* How can you ask a child to understand something that makes no sense at all?

Of course, I would love nothing more than to go back and do things differently. I could have told someone at school, a teacher or any adult. I could have called 911. Maybe I simply didn't know I had a choice. Without understanding options existed, I could do nothing other than block it out of my mind.

Children have an innate desire for happiness, so they will always move towards it. They simply *are* happiness and see only good existing in the world. Through these eyes, I continued trying to be happy. Something so horrific would never happen again, right? I tried to make whatever sense I could of it since no one was providing any explanation. School was teaching me right and wrong by the ways the Lord cared for his people, so I knew this was all wrong, but I had not the slightest clue who I was up against. No idea who this person was. *Where did he come from? Why is he here, tormenting our lives?* Nothing made sense to me. Nothing was ever explained. I was a child, trying to make sense of an adult's world.

But, now in my own adult life, I finally understand. The truth all along was: it doesn't make sense. Not in the adult's world. Not even in any world. There's nothing to make sense of.

...

Down the street from our Mozart home lived Ian's mother, Luciana. She never quite liked me. In fact, she hated me. No, she loathed me, and she provided me with countless reasons why. I resembled my mother and she hated my mom. I wasn't Ian's real daughter anyway. Whatever her issue was with me, I never really understood.

It made sense that Caleb would have little to keep him busy when I was gone to my father's for the weekends, so these weekends became his time with Grandma. Yet, on the occasional Friday when Ian would destroy any opportunity for me to leave with my Dad, I went with Caleb to visit with a grandmother who hated the sight of me.

Caleb and I would take a short walk down the street with Ian and once we arrived, he would drop our bags in her bedroom. I remember one time when she greeted Caleb and turned her wrinkled, makeup dusted cheek at me, I responded by wandering off to the dining room and curiously roaming through the bottom shelves of the china cabinet finding trinkets, tiny silverware, and boxes caked with a thick layer of dust that concealed various types of knick-knacks inside. I wandered off into my own world of imagination and pretended I was going to find something that would be life-changing. I eventually noticed that I'd been left alone for a long, uninterrupted time. I quickly put all the things away that I had scrounged through and rushed off in search of Caleb.

I dashed into the kitchen where I saw him sitting at the table eating. Grandma was standing at the counter as I ran in and shot me a sharp look.

"Walk," she said. My happy feelings all quickly went away as she set a familiar tone.

I slowly walked to the kitchen table where Caleb was sitting and climbed onto the seat next to him while waiting for my food. I played with the clear plastic cover that lay on top of a bright yellow cloth.

"Here," she said, pushing food in front of me. I glanced at Caleb's plate and noticed we were eating two different things; something that would never have happened at home. We always ate the same thing and if you didn't like what was for dinner then you just stayed hungry and possibly even went to bed early for pouting and disagreeing. That thought quickly left my mind and I reached for my spoon.

As we were finishing, Caleb and I jumped off the metal chairs and headed to the living room to play. As I followed him out of the kitchen, I was stopped by her hand on my shoulder. Without a word, she turned me round and lightly pushed me back towards my seat. I sat down just waiting for her to speak, but she said nothing.

Caleb, noticing I wasn't behind him, came running back with a confused look to see me at the table. "C'mon!" he said.

Appearing at a loss, I remained speechless. Before I could say a word she quickly scooped him up and walked with him to the living room. I sat at the table in silence listening to the television they were watching.

I guessed I was in trouble for running. I didn't really know. I had assumed that she would come to get me after some time, but she never did. I grew sad and extremely bored as the light outside disappeared, the blue of the sky fading to black. I quietly walked to the living room past the dark hallway to see Caleb sitting on her lap as they watched TV from the single Lazy Boy recliner.

"Can I get up now?" I quietly mumbled. She swung around in her chair.

"What?" she said.

A little louder I repeated, "Can I get up now?"

"It's time to get ready for bed," she sighed as she turned off the television.

Caleb and I took our baths, brushed our hair, and put on nighttime clothes. I climbed on top of a tall, large bed and watched the bulky TV box with metal antennas that was sitting on top of the dark wooden dresser. I waited for Caleb to join me but became distracted watching Spanish game shows that I didn't understand. I began to wonder where he was. I leaped off the bed to find him sitting in the recliner with her again. When I tried to sit on the plastic covered floral sofa to join them, she interrupted with, "You, you go to bed."

Getting frustrated, I mustered up some courage, "I don't want to."

She abruptly swung around her chair, stood up and sat Caleb down, "You hit the sack!" She pointed at me, then snatched my arm and turned me around, jerking me straight to the room.

"Hit the sack!" her voice shrieked. I understood her tone, but I couldn't understand the words over her heavy Spanish accent.

Confused, I responded with, "What sock?" My question only made her angrier.

Once she saw to it that I was in bed, she turned off the light and closed the door, leaving me in the darkness. I lay scared, for I was still using night lights. A few moments later, after I'd convinced myself that a monster would not grab my foot, I quietly crept off the bed, being careful not to make a peep. I gently opened the door which allowed for the flashing television light to beam into the room. I drew the door open to my liking, crawled back under the stiff sheets that smelled of her awful perfume and fell asleep, gazing at the bright blue light.

...

Summers in the Chicago suburbs had their perks and blissful freedom from being inside. I believe I was fortunate enough to have grown up in the age where swimming in the pool, playing tag outside, climbing trees and riding bikes throughout the neighborhood was the example of an accomplished summer day. The excitement in the sun became even more memorable as Caleb and I became older and were allowed to continue our fun outside at night when the lightning bugs floated in the air.

The darkness would awaken the fireflies and the night time atmosphere sparkled with glowing green lights. Of course, we rummaged through the kitchen cupboards to find the perfect jar to place them in. It never worked, though. Every time you opened the jar to catch one, another one would fly right out. I realized my jar never quite measured up to the bright, illuminating jars I'd seen in movies.

Caleb and I spent many hot summer days riding bikes around the neighborhood and were lured by the excitement of stopping at some of the scariest houses around the block. We pretended that the tall, long driveways in the alleys were ramps and we would zoom down them. We would go to the "Pear Store," a spot down the block where our imagination was in full force and three mature pear trees hugged the sidewalk near an apartment building. One of us would snatch up as many as we could while the other kept a lookout for the adults who had yelled at us just days before for stealing their fruit.

Fun was found in the true simplicity of being a child. Walking down the sidewalk, we approached a huge black and brown dog which I now know was a Rottweiler. Loving dogs as much as I did, I decided I would be bold and pet it. I walked right up to it, calling it by all sorts of cute names and making all sorts of cute noises.

I turned towards Caleb, "C'mon, there's nothing to be afraid of." I spoke with confidence as I approached the dog.

Caleb remained a careful distance behind me, unconvinced, and rightfully so. I slowly stuck my finger out to pet it and *SNAP!* that dog chomped on my tiny hand.

"Shit!" I yelled. It was the first time I remember swearing.

"Dammit!" I shouted. "Get away! Get away!" I yelled as I ran back home wailing, my arms in the air. "Stupid dog!"

With the daylong exhilaration and exerted energy, we ultimately came back inside. It was not because anyone called for us. It was only because it was getting darker. The outside sky turned to dusk and the sunlight faded. We went inside to eat only after the appetite we had ignored for so long made it essential.

For the most part, I ate horribly as a child, simply horrible. I ate the kind of food they talk about today on television, radio and magazines as being known for causing obesity, cancer, heart attacks and high cholesterol. It was the only food you could find in our cabinets. Such a thing as "healthy" was barely known to us. Velveeta mac and cheese, chicken pot pies, or pizza bagels for dinner was a pretty regular affair. Breakfast consisted of sausage biscuits, frozen waffles, frozen stacks of pancakes, microwaved bacon, microwaved sausage, and syrup; lots and lots of syrup. See, just simply horrible.

Occasionally, however, there were home-cooked meals. Mom made the juiciest pork chops and all her cakes, especially her cheesecakes, were gone the same hour after coming out of the oven. She would make something called beer bread which I always thought was gross, yet I never minded sipping from Ian's Corona once in a while when he let me. It usually made Mom really angry, and I didn't like to make Mom angry.

When she'd be in the kitchen baking, she would prop me up on the counter and let me lick the mixing ladles, the spoon and the bowl. I always wanted the leftovers in the dishes that were headed for the sink, especially the sticky white rice from the bottom of her rice cooker. I never had to ask her for it. While I was in the middle of watching Seinfeld, she'd hand me the large silver bowl without a word and go back into the kitchen. I would sit on the floor, staring at the television with a large metal spoon in my small hands, scrapping up the crunchy, chewy pieces of rice stuck at the bottom. I was glad no one else wanted any.

However, more often than not there were Wendy's runs for double bacon cheeseburgers, White Castle crave cases, and every child's favorite: The Happy Meal.

Ian would arrive back from picking up our choice of take-out and it was on. Omar, Junior, young girly-me and little blonde headed Caleb would dive into the grub, grabbing whatever we could snatch up. You got what you got and that was that, but please someone leave the ones without cheese. Caleb hated cheese.

Being the only female sibling made for a diverse up-bringing. I would play hours of Mario Kart on Nintendo 64 and sometimes Crash Bandicoot on the PlayStation if Omar and Junior were nice enough to let me get a turn, or if I cried for one. I would wrestle them, and every time I seemed to be winning, they seemed to respect me more. But because they were bigger than I was, I usually ended up getting hurt. Sometimes they would hush me up if the hurt wasn't too bad, but other times I left crying for Mom. I didn't mean to get them into trouble, but that's usually what ended up happening. Like the time Omar said he just wanted to look at my loose tooth and then yanked it right out of my mouth. Mom would yell at them for "rough-housing" with me and told them to leave me alone. But I didn't want that either.

I enjoyed trying to beat them up and having them throw me up into the air so I could do the "Pocahontas", as I splashed into the swimming pool. I also enjoyed more girly play, like dressing my Barbies and making them mommies to the little dolls who lived in my Kelly Pop-Up Play House.

My memory is flooded with hours upon hours of time I spent with my siblings, but I can recall little-to-none with Mom. I don't remember seeing much of her and definitely never playing with her. In fact, I do recall wondering where she was on many occasions and then feeling sad. It felt like a long time had passed since I had last seen her. I knew I would get to see her at bedtime though when she always came with my goodnight kiss.

I disliked how little she was ever around, but also knew it was because she worked the night shifts at the Swedish Covenant hospital as a receptionist. She would sleep during the middle of the day and wake at 9:30 PM. If I could, I laid awake in my room, listening to her getting ready. She kept the same routine my whole life, so I knew when she was almost done and when she was about to leave. I often fell asleep before I heard her go, but the nights I could remain awake, I waited for her to creak open my bedroom door and soothe me with her goodnight kisses and hugs. I was happiest when I got the good stuff and had those moments of her time. She always had a way of making me feel special, being the last one she said goodnight to.

Some nights, I would slumber off and would wake up right in the middle of the back door slamming shut. I would jolt out of bed and search for anything that flashed or was bright enough to see from a distance. If I couldn't find any sort of toy that fit this description, I would just turn on my bedroom light—this was my least favorite option. So if I ever found the right light, I kept it close to my nightstand and only used it for these moments.

Nights when I was prepared, I would stand at my window staring at the backyard, eagerly waiting to see her walk out the back door. She would drive out of the garage, into the alley in her white SUV and turn left, stopping at the fence and waiting to see if I would show. I never knew how she caught on or how this became "our thing", but she and I knew it was. When I saw her stop, I would begin to flash my beacon of light. Under the orange alley light, I could see her looking up as she smiled and waved at me. Using a small flashing light instead of the entire bedroom light made it easier for me to see her glowing smile from the distance. We waved at one another for a little longer than normal, blowing kisses at each other from across the yard. After a brief moment of unspoken affection, she would drive off down the alley. I stared at her car until she turned onto the street and I could no longer see her. When her rear lights were entirely out of sight, I stayed at my window alone in the darkness of my room and whispered, "Dear Lord, please keep her safe."

...

The First Return

OUR NEIGHBORHOOD was alive with diversity and city-skirt culture. During the age where block parties were big events, I would wander around the food and games, then join the kids I thought were having the most fun.

From time to time, I would get caught up with the older kids I knew from the block and take the 10-minute walk down the alley to the convenience store just to buy some peach-O's. Only *parts* of our neighborhood were safe. Staying out past dark became riskier as years passed and the neighborhood changed. Over time, I came to know my surroundings well enough to recognize every face and match it to every home.

Some of those faces belonged to our neighbors. One was a Spanish lady with a perfectly clean home and a Rottweiler. She mostly kept to herself. I barely ever saw her outside of the summer months when she watered her lawn and let her wild pup out.

Our other neighbor was a Hispanic family. They owned

two large fluffy grey huskies with crystal blue eyes. On countless occasions, Caleb and I would stir them up from the other side of the fence. One of the daughters, Isabella, would occasionally baby-sit me. She's memorable in my mind because of her bright green eyes giving her the nickname Buttercup, as in Buttercup from the *Power Puff Girls*. She even had the short, black hair and spunky attitude to match.

Our families did not interact very often. On the rare occasions when I needed a sitter, I would go over to their house and play in a room in the back of the house. In it were mountains upon mountains of large, small, and medium-sized stuffed animals stacked high on top of a very tall bed. The animals were piled so high they nearly covered the entire window behind them. The bed was saturated with various fluffy animals, so I was in a fluffy heaven. Needless to say, I spent several hours there.

When I had my fill of fluff, I would sit in their tiny kitchen at the small iron table and stare out the window into the next house: our house. *Well, there it is*, I thought, finally being able to see from the other side into our own bedroom. The windows were no further apart than two or three feet. Looking down I could see the thin sidewalk trailing below; only wide enough to walk in a single-file line. That window looked into a bedroom I used to have before I was moved upstairs. I thought of how I had stared out from the other side many terrified nights, wondering what was over here. I thought of how I had sat in that room, shaking with fear, listening to Ian's rage and Mom's cries. Sometimes I sat alone. Other times I was with Caleb.

As I sat staring at our home, I started to think about fear and what it truly meant. Like an illness, it seeped into my bones;

making itself comfortable and me uncomfortable. Fear became a regular uncertainty that dictated everything I did. I could see it on everyone's worried faces, heard it in everyone's trembling voice and recognized it in everyone's lack of natural behavior. Everything always uncertain. We all became different people when he was around. This fear created distance between Mom and me, obstructing our relationship because of his deranged needs.

We had to change when he was present. I knew I couldn't speak naturally with Mom. Much of the communication we had in his presence came through our eyes, body language or short, hesitant words.

We all played our role. Mom remained obedient, agreeable, and avoided long conversations. She forced a smile at the dinner table and laughed carefully. Then, when he left, the tension would disappear. We could be silly again, be playful, and laugh hysterically for hours. I noticed how all of our smiles were packed away and stuffed in a box, like a part of us that never existed when he was home. I felt the fear that she silently spoke and behaved accordingly. I followed her lead, almost as if I were learning a second language. Whenever I started to lose my cover, her eyes would grow wide saying *"stop it"* or *"get it together."*

I knew she loved me. She was protecting me.

...

Part of my school's mission was to guide each child to walk with the Lord. The pastor would give a speech every month to remind us how important this was. He let each student know that in order to begin your relationship with God, you had to ask him to come into your heart; to save yourself and to be able to ask for forgiveness when you needed it.

I grew up listening to stories of the Bible every morning for 7 years. I listened to stories of God's good grace, his ability to heal and help those who suffered. I especially enjoyed the story about the fish and the bread. As the messages flooded my mind, I kept asking the question, *Why was this happening to us?*

I carried the fear from home to school. One day, when the pastor bid us to ask the Lord to come into our hearts, I decided I would do just that. *Maybe this was all because of something I had done. Maybe this would help.*

My class stood up from the pews, and I waited till each row was dismissed before following. Walking down the hallway, I debated, *Should I? Should I ask?* It seemed terrifying. I was raised believing that the Lord has great power and control in the decisions of our lives, so what would he decide for me?

After my class returned to the classroom and everyone took their seats, Mrs. Hughes directed us to begin reading quietly. I sat at my desk, thinking, not even turning a page of my book. *I will, I will ask.*

I walked to the front of the classroom and stood at the end of her desk waiting for her acknowledgement.

"Yes, Monica?" The pastor's wife, Mrs. Hughes, said softly.

"I want to ask. Umm. I want to ask for the Lord to come into my heart." I mumbled every word. Staring at the ground, I was nervous and barely audible.

"Say again dear?" She smiled and leaned in closer toward me.

I repeated, "I want to ask you to pray with me."

"For what dear?" Her eyes widened.

"For God to come into my heart." I was relieved to have asked and could finally look up at her. She scooted close in her chair and reached for my hands, placing them in hers. I felt the cold brush of her bracelet and could see the dark veins in her fingers. With her kind, shining blue eyes upon me she said, "Let's pray."

We bowed our heads and closed our eyes. She whispered a longer prayer than I was expecting, but I remained with my head bowed and eyes closed.

When she was finished, she brought her face within inches of mine and peered over her large golden glasses, whispering, "God is with you wherever you go. He will always be with you." She hugged me tight and I latched my arms around her. I smiled, went back to my seat and took a deep breath. Feeling relieved, I opened my book.

Home was never spoken about, but I had great relief knowing the Lord was now on my side.

...

October 1997
Winter was approaching. The air became chilled and the bright sunlight of the day didn't stay for nearly as long as expected.

We had a day to ourselves, the kind that brought immense joy and relief from not playing the roles Ian always expected. Mom took Caleb and me out to do some errands. We spent our time looking through clothes and toys.

While I was rummaging, a tiny book caught my eye. I can't tell you what it was about or why it grabbed my attention, but I thought it was as cute as button. I wanted it. When I asked

Mom if I could have it, she happily tossed it into the cart and a smile lit up my face.

We left and on the way home we stopped to pick up a pizza. We arrived before Ian, and I went into my room to sit on my bed and admire my tiny, cute book. Then Mom walked in.

She sat on the bed next to me. "Don't let him see this. Okay? Hide it somewhere."

"Okay," I smiled. She squeezed me, kissed the top of my head, and returned to the kitchen.

"Now come eat!"

I glanced around my bedroom. *Where could I hide this?* I then picked up my pillow and placed it underneath. *Perfect.*

A few moments later, as Mom was starting to serve Caleb and me pizza, Ian arrived home. Mom stood at the kitchen counter opening the pizza box and he wasted no time in shattering the good mood of our day.

I felt the fear beginning to spark as I listened to him question her about where she had gotten the money for the pizza, for shopping. He wanted to know where we had been all day. Remaining simple and calm as usual, Mom replied sweetly, but this time it seemed to have no effect. Something was different.

He became enraged and began to yell at her. As he grew louder and more incensed, he forced her into their bedroom and slammed the door. I stood in front of the television with Caleb by my side. My appetite was lost, and I could no longer focus on anything other than the screaming from their bedroom.

Tension began rising without any relief in sight, growing as he dominated her every word and demanded that she give him answers. The same fear I had felt on the worst of nights began trickling in, numbing my entire body. My feet felt locked to the floor. I was in a complete void with a sharp focus on nothing other than his loud, violent words. The TV seemed mute and I paid no attention to the slice of pizza still dangling in my hand. All my senses stopped for Mom.

Yelling struck into screaming, then screaming ignited into cursing. All control was being lost. I couldn't move. I had never stood so close to his violence. I had always been more distant when he exploded. As I stood outside their door, I was drenched in fear as I listened to his hateful words when suddenly ...

There was a painful, startlingly loud explosion that tore through the house. Terror rushed through me and I began screaming. Frantic, I could hear Mom and Ian dreadfully panicking from inside the room.

"Ohhh, no! NO! NO! NO! NO! NO! You're bleeding!" he piercingly shrieked, "You're bleeding!".

"Ian, no...no. I'm fine!" I heard Mom's voice shout.

"Ohhh, NO! NO! NO! You're bleeding!", Ian cried out again, "NO! Nooooooo!" Madness consumed the air with Ian's loss of control. He was frantic.

"Mmmahhhhhhhh!!!" Mom emitted a terribly wrenching cry that rang throughout the neighborhood.

"Pray!" He shouted, "PRAY!"

"Iaaaan! Stop!" Her voice was frightened. She begged him, "Stop!"

"Give it to me! Give it to me!" he demanded.

"Ian STOP! You're scaring my babies!" she cried. Then within seconds, the bedroom door sprang open.

"Ahhhhhhh!" she screamed as she bolted out the room and fled for her life. I looked down the hall and saw her racing to the front door, holding her right hand in the air as she disappeared into the darkness.

She had been shot in the hand.

A second later, Ian dashed out of the bedroom in hysteria with wild eyes and saw me standing there. He rushed over to me with panic filling his face.

"Which way did she go!" he demanded.

"I don't know," I softly cried.

"Don't you lie to me."

Without a word, I pointed to the back door and watched as he immediately dashed down the stairs and outside the door, running in the wrong direction.

Flushed into a stupor, Caleb and I stood crying. Mom and Ian had left. Only the echoing silence remained.

Then my mind draws into blackness. It is a way, I believe, that my body tries to shield me from my own awful feelings in that moment.

Years later, I was informed Mom had fled to the neighbor's house and demanded that someone go get her children. In her 911 call, she told the dispatcher she believed Ian would kill us.

Memory then returns to the moment I was being rushed into to the neighbor's house, blinded by bright shining lights. Mom was frantically crying and screaming as she sat in their living room, surrounded by the Hispanic family. Everyone was in a terrified state of alarm. I stood back with one of the daughters as I watched Mom screaming in pain and the family trying to ease her hysteria and stop the bleeding.

I pulled at the daughter's arm, "Please! Let her be okay!" She said nothing. Her eyes were drowning with panic as she held me close to her side.

With not the slightest idea of what was to come and no

understanding of what had just happened, I became numb.

...

I've recalled this haunting memory countless times in my life: hearing the screams, feeling the fear and analyzing every moment of the day. It wasn't until twenty years later, at the age of twenty-five, that I finally received an explanation about what happened that night.

When we returned home, Mom received flowers that were addressed to Ian for his birthday. The card that came with it was signed by a woman named Gloria. The flowers had been initially delivered to Luciana's house down the street, but she directed the delivery man to Ian's real address. When Ian arrived, Mom questioned him about the flowers and the card.

...

That night left us frail with an imprint of terror greater than I could have ever fathomed

Days later, I was awakened in the middle of the night. My Tia Carlita quickly turned on the closet light as Mom began pulling out clothes from the dresser and stuffing them into luggage. Both of them moved quickly.

Sleepy and still incoherent, I asked, "Where are we going?" I stood on the bed being dressed by my Tia. Caleb, whose eyes were still closed, sat at the end of his bed.

"We have to go," Mom whispered.

"Yeah we're gonna go on a trip!" Tia batted her lashes and smiled. I felt the worry behind her voice as she helped

Mom rush us out of the house and into the dark silence of the neighborhood. We raced towards the car across the street. Once we were buckled in, they slammed the car doors and immediately sped off.

Ian was too familiar with Mom's family; he knew where every one of them lived. But in a distant part of Chicago was Mom's own tia and tio whom Ian knew nothing of.

It was close to sunrise when we arrived at their house. We stayed for the next several weeks, embracing the first peaceful nights of sleep in a long time.

During those days, I slept in a strange bed in a strange home. I didn't watch TV, play, or talk much. Instead, I wandered aimlessly for hours in their basement, trying to entertain myself as Mom rested in the upstairs bedroom with her hand wrapped in bandages. Caleb came and left. I don't know where he went, but I was alone and missed him.

But after that short time away, we returned to the Mozart house. There was an unusual feeling left in the air. In those few short weeks, the house had already become unfamiliar. Something felt eerie and unsettling. It no longer gave a greeting of welcome but served as a reminder of the night we had endured.

It was just the three of us. Ian stayed down the street with his mother. He had lost his job at the police department, lost his wife, lost his children, and now had lost his home. Eventually, he grew remorseful.

He called Mom, pleading for her forgiveness. He called her and begged her to take him back. He told her that he missed her, that he missed the children. He said that he didn't know what he was thinking, that he didn't mean anything he had said before. He assured her that he would change, she could trust him, and he would never do it again. He promised.

Soon, Mom retracted her restraining order, dropped the charges, and did not testify in court against him. She left Ian with no punishment for what he had done.

With all of his remorseful, sweet apologies, Ian and Mom reconciled. He came back to the house in December and appeared gravely apologetic. He appeared to be kind and thankful to be home. *Was he different?* I couldn't tell.

Yet tension seemed to linger in his every step. Even if we had a peaceful day when no angry words were exchanged and nothing happened, I would awake out of a deep sleep for the slightest noise. A car in the alley, a siren through the neighborhood; I was on constant alert. I worried about the next terrible moment that would come. Ian had already taught me there would always be a next time, and I knew that he was capable of far worse actions than any of us could imagine.

After his return, silence was stuck in the air. I wasn't quite sure how to act with him anymore. *How do I play after what happened? Am I supposed to be nice? Was he still bad?* I noticed no one seemed willing to act and play the family roles anymore.

I could paint no picture of how any of this was to be resolved. I was gravely confused by his return yet saw that no one rebelled against his presence. Although everyone looked dreary, we all went along with the entire, uncomfortable acceptance of his return. The effort to pretend was minimal. I couldn't hide how I felt, and he could see the fear written on my face.

Ian's tense kindness started to make me think we had just given him back all his control. Although I kept my distance, he didn't allow it for too long.

"This is mine." He caught me off guard as he wrapped my

curly ponytail tightly around his hand. I stood still, his hand controlling my next move.

"This is mine," he repeated. After a pause that was too long with his hand still wrapped onto my hair, he eventually smirked and then smiled. I followed his lead.

"No, it's not," I said, allowing my fear to break.

"Yes, it is. This is mineee." He was beginning to tease.

"No, it's mine!" I laughed, and he slowly let go. I pushed at his belly and he swooped me up. He flung me onto the recliner chair and began tickling me. I laughed even more as his moustache brushed my cheek. We were playing? Was that, okay?

Our playfulness was brief, and we both laughed with exhaustion. Strangely, playfully arguing about to whom did my hair belong became our thing.

Sometimes I couldn't tell if he was playing or not. Often, he waited for a long time before he smirked to indicate he was joking. Many other times, I thought he was serious. It seemed as if once he sensed my fear, he would become playful.

When I became older, he seemed to purposely start this playful banter at the worst times. If I was truly angry, upset or afraid, I did not feel like laughing, but I would play along anyway. I knew what it meant not to. Eventually, I learned to force the same smile that Mom did, even when I was screaming inside.

I couldn't understand why he was back, or why Mom had allowed it. He sold his remorseful act for the first few weeks, but slowly slithered back into his futile-self. I saw him begin to unleash his pent-up anger, little by little, about everything that had been taken from him that night. He became resentful and blamed Mom for provoking him. She had caused him to lose his job at the police department and was the reason he had to look for work now.

This was *her* fault.

...

April 2002

I came downstairs to find Mom and Ian in the living room and noticed something black strapped to Ian's ankle. Naively, I asked Mom what was on his leg.

"Oh, Papi just hurt his leg and this is going to make it feel better," Mom replied sweetly.

"Oh, okay."

I thought nothing more about it until Ian's two children from his first marriage came to our house. Veronica was a six-teen-year-old fair skinned girl with large brown eyes and long, soft brown hair. As a young girl, she was the 'pretty' I wanted to be. I was excited when I knew she was coming over because it meant I could brush her long waves. But the grooming stopped the day I tangled a brush into her hair and it was impossible to remove. As Veronica became aware that the brush was stuck, I slowly backed away while others came to help her and assess the damage. I felt so awful to have ruined something so pretty that I never asked to brush her hair again.

Her brother, Dylan, was older than me by a couple of years, but not old enough to think I was an annoying young kid. The older kids, Omar, Junior and Veronica, would be talking inside while Dylan and I played outside. We were on the sidewalk throwing rocks when the black ankle bracelet was mentioned.

"Yeah, Mommy said Papi hurt his leg."

"What!" Dylan replied.

"What?"

"He didn't hurt his leg!" he exclaimed.

My ears were perked, "What do you mean?"

"It's an ankle bracelet." Dylan explained. He turned me around and pointed down the sidewalk, "If he even goes to the end down there, the police will be here and take him to jail."

"Really?" I said, trying to make sense.

"Yeah! They told you he hurt his foot?" He laughed and continued looking for bugs in the dirt.

"Yeah." I paused in sadness and felt hurt realizing Mom had lied to me. I then began to wonder about what other lies she may have told me.

. . .

Summer 2002

It was summer and we were on vacation for the next three months. A couple of days after Veronica and Dylan left, my Tia Carlita and four cousins came over. *Finally, some girls!* They spent the entire day with me, laughing, talking, styling my hair and playing dress up. As night came, I begged Mom for my youngest cousin, Imelia to sleep over. She and I were closest in age and would play Barbies for hours. But Mom said no. It was always a no when it came to anyone spending the night.

Before my cousins left, the five of us spent a moment talking in my room, all of us huddled on my tiny twin-sized bed.

"You doing okay?" my oldest cousin asked.

"Yeah, why?" I said.

"Well, you know about what happened to Ian." Imelia asked.

"Oh." Embarrassed, I answered, "Yeah, I found out." Pausing, I then asked, "Do you know why he has to wear it?"

"Well, I heard he got caught with drugs," she whispered. They continued to talk among themselves, disputing the details, but my ears left the conversation. I let her words digest. I didn't know what drugs were. All I knew was what everyone had told me: drugs are bad. Something I was always taught to stay away from. That was the extent of what I knew, so I couldn't think any further. I couldn't think anything at all. I didn't know what to make of it. Something was terribly wrong, and no one was telling me the truth.

I wanted to know what was happening. Mom and Ian were behaving so oddly that I eventually started listening to their conversations. I crept around the corner, remaining silent and still as they spoke in hushed tones. I learned that Ian had been arrested for transporting and selling drugs and that he hadn't hesitated to sell out the other dealers in order to catch himself a break. But that meant we could all be in danger, because those people might seek revenge. Mom sounded worried and I began to understand why, even when Ian wasn't around, she seemed on edge.

I never let her know what I knew. I figured she had her reasons to hide it from me. I also didn't want to disappoint them by revealing just how much their cover-ups had failed.

...

Nights later, I was picked up from my bed in the middle of

the night and carried to the living room. I sat on the couch, noticing the entire family was sitting around the room and only a single candle flickered on the coffee table.

Everyone was awake, particularly Mom and Ian who appeared to be on high alert as they paced up and down the hallway and quietly argued to one another, yet weren't arguing *with* one another.

Mom sat with us, seemingly nervous, waiting for Ian to return. He disappeared into the darkness, keeping close to every window.

We waited in silence as the warm orange streetlight shined through the drapes, illuminating our faces. I began to question what was happening when a sudden noise broke through the silence. Gunshots were being fired on the neighborhood streets. We all jumped in our seats and listened intently. The sound was a rapid explosion and then, nothing. All was still. We waited for the next sound that would tell us what was happening outside.

A car alarm sounded and rang for the next several minutes. Nothing followed. No shouts, no voices in the distance, no sirens. After a few moments, it all seemed to have passed. I couldn't help but think, *Was this our warning?*

Because of his cooperation with the drug arrest and giving the court other people's names, Ian only earned himself a period of house arrest and four years in prison.

...

The yelling jolted me from my sleep. The same familiar fear began rushing in. Coming from the floor below me were shouts and screams. Ian was yelling, screaming vulgar words that I hadn't heard for a while. He wasn't stopping, and I could feel him spiraling out of control. I heard the doors downstairs open and slam. Each one was louder than the last. With each slamming door my body tightened as I lay in my bed, helplessly waiting for the next noise.

Already terrified of what could possibly be happening, my imagination made it worse by sending horrible images to my eyes. I was left to fill in the gaps only with what I could hear. I listened intently. I could hear him yelling with hostility and swearing at her, her desperate stream of cries struggling to escape his shouts.

The screeching of her shoes on the tile floor and carpet told me she was being dragged and the sound of her voice slowly traveled from one room to another.

"Stop!" she yelled. "Stop! Let go! Let me go!" I knew he was hurting her. I could hear her struggling and being banged up against the doors, the vibrations shooting through the walls. She was resisting. The random shatter of falling objects made it difficult to hear what Ian was saying. I knew he was dragging her all the way through the house and I imagined it was by her hair. He continued through the front door and outside down the stone entrance. I heard her tumbling. I knew she was hurt.

The pain in her voice forced me into tears, deeper with every painful plea she emitted. He then walked back inside and slammed the door. I listened with my ear to the floor and heard him talking under his breath. Mom was still shouting from outside.

Her cries from the front door became softer. Quieter. And in a short time, nothing at all. Silence took over the night. I crawled back to bed and I lay stiff, thinking. *Would she stay there? Where would she go? Will she be okay for the night?* Knowing I could do nothing, I simply spoke to the Lord and prayed our neighbor would be helpful again and take her inside.

Staring at the ceiling, allowing hours to pass, I replayed everything I had just heard. The echoes in my mind made me feel as though I could still hear them. The silence brought no peace to my mind or to my heart. Tears continued to pour down my cheeks. I waited, prepared, for any other terror he might bring in the night.

...

August 2003

Between the two of them, I assume they had a long, difficult conversation concerning what should happen next. I'm not sure if anything was planned, since nothing in our lives seemed to follow any considerable level of thought or organization. I don't believe I was considered. I never felt like I was. To me, Mom considered Ian more important. There was no way it could be about the kids. Ian's situation was becoming dangerous and had surpassed his control. It was time for change.

The school year had just begun, and I was incredibly excited to have moved up into my new uniform for 5th grade. I had long been ready to get out of the old one. Soon after the start of the school year, Mom decided to ask me a question on the way home.

"So, how would you feel about moving?" I could tell she was attempting to be nonchalant and perhaps didn't even like the question herself.

"I don't want to move!" I panicked. "I have my school here and my friends here. I don't want to move!"

I wanted to trade my home life, not my school life. My small Baptist school had become my second home, my second family. I had spent my life there since I could form words and feelings.

They were my best friends, my teachers and my pastor. They were the people who had taught me to read, write, spell, and had guided me with morals, religion and simple manners. They had taught me how to be a good human being. Now I was being forced to give them all up.

I soon realized Mom's question was only a polite way of providing me time to process what had already been decided. A warning, really, rather than any sort of genuine intent to understand how I would truly feel about moving.

The arrangements began. The boxes started to gather, and I was asked on many occasions to have my room in perfect order because people would be coming to see it. Everyone assured me this was a good thing and everything would be great. That it would be an exciting new start for our family. I was told I would be in a school like I had seen in my television shows where I would no longer have to wear a uniform but my own clothes. Perhaps it was because of my initial reaction, but no one bothered to say anything further. I had no other conversations with anyone about the move beyond the question from the car that day.

Our house sold in 2003 to a family I never met. Then, things started moving quickly. My room was packed up in boxes galore. Even the enormous junk-filled basement was empty; it was the one place I could always search to find new things that were either misplaced or forgotten since the 70's. It was completely wiped out. I roamed around the empty spaces while people loaded the truck, recalling both good and bad memories.

They had rented a massively long U-Haul truck which, by the end of the day, was filled front to back and bottom to top. The bird cage with our two parakeets would have surely been shaken up, so Caleb and I were asked to stand inside the truck and hold it while they drove us to our new home.

In Cedar Forest on Alenda Street was a two-story red barn-looking house with an attached garage. We would call it home for the next eight years. I thought it was horrendous. It was truly ugly and looked as though pigs and chickens should be roaming the yard. *Why were we moving here again?* I knew I would never get an answer, but assumed it had something to do with the night we heard gunshots from the street.

During this transition, the first decision I was asked to make was to choose my room. My choice was between the large room in the back of the house on the second floor or the smaller room right next to it. I chose the larger.

The walls were a faded summer yellow with two warm wood shelves on the wall. The space was half the size of my old room and not nearly as bright. It didn't seem like any children had lived here either. Everything was old and dusty. The second decision I had was to choose the color of my room and the wallpaper border that would line the ceiling. I was a vibrant child, so I chose a bright purple paint for the walls and butterfly border. Each butterfly had crazy patterns and colors in their wings.

The day we moved in, I wasted no time. I tried to get excited about the change, since it was going to happen with or without my approval. So I focused on my new room, and while everyone else was in the living room relaxing and eating pizza, I was in my yellow room, unpacking boxes and neatly placing all my things where I wanted them to be. I was determined to have it done that same day, but the furniture wasn't set up, so I only did as much as I could. After I'd spent hours decorating and hanging my clothes, I crashed on the mattress in the middle of the floor. I woke up the next morning to coffee cake for breakfast. It was given to us from the new neighbors as a welcome to the neighborhood.

Then I started getting ready for school. It was my first time attending a school in my own clothes, so naturally I had no idea what to wear. I wildly searched my newly arranged closet to eventually decide on a sporty blue shirt with the numbers "69" on the front along with some blue-grey stretchy jeans. I thought I was so cool, like Lizzie McGuire and her creative style. I waited at the bus stop which was just in front of our new house. I had never done that before, and waited for the large yellow bus that was coming to pick me up.

When it arrived, I hurried on, and with no idea where to sit, I chose the first seat I saw. Later on, I learned that the front seat was the loser seat.

When I arrived at school, I was guided to my classroom by a teacher who greeted me at the bus stop. She introduced herself as Mrs. Crum, and I followed behind her. She led me down a bright narrow hallway to my classroom where I would be picking up my 5th grade year.

In my previous classroom I sat in an all-white cubicle and worked independently all day, only speaking to the teacher if I needed help. There was nothing on the walls other than bible verses and songs. My days there were quiet, and I worked to the sound of shuffling papers and clicks on a keyboard.

At my old school, everyone worked at a different pace. We all worked on different assignments and in different grades. Naturally, I knew it would take some time to adjust to my new school, but I took excessively longer than most.

I sat quietly at a wooden desk while the teacher sat at hers in front of the classroom. As the other students started coming in, I became nervous. They all seemed to know what to do and where everything was. They placed their coats in cubbies, found their seat, and took out some sort of book I later learned was an assignment note book.

After everyone was seated, Mrs. Crum called me to the front and, as an introduction, had the class try to guess my name.

"This is our new classmate. Can anyone guess her name? I'll give you a hint; It's a name from *Friends*!" she said. They came up with some ridiculous names, and I felt more embarrassed with every turn they took. No one was guessing *Monica*.

Eventually she gave them the answer and asked me some questions. I was extremely nervous and probably said something entirely generic, for I had no idea how to speak in front of other people and I wasn't used to people asking about me. It made me uncomfortable.

When the embarrassment was over, I returned to my seat. *What is Friends?* The room was filled with information: books on the shelves, crafting tools everywhere, projects left on the table behind me, and boards for your behavior. I felt entirely out of my element.

I was lost and soon, frustrated. I had no idea how to function here, so I kept silent and observed everything. Every. Single. Thing. I didn't understand the social norms; didn't grasp the subjects or the social cliques and their obsession with Abercrombie, American Eagle and Hollister clothes. I soon realized I wasn't up to speed on my math or computer skills, my history knowledge, or my science understanding. I went from feeling like one of the smartest students, a teacher's pet even, to one of the dumbest. I was constantly teased for my silence, for my clothes, and for my bad grades.

As the year passed, I began to feel inferior and eventually dreaded school. The bus rides, sitting alone at lunch, and the ridicule that came from not being able to answer any of the questions when I was called on was horrible. I hated every part of it.

There was a small sigh of relief whenever we were released to gym, music, art or recess. Those were the moments I didn't need to think. I liked it that way. Simply standing in the bathroom line was relaxing too. I quickly identified the moments where nothing would be expected of me and enjoyed them for the brief peace they brought.

At recess, I walked the playground alone while everyone else huddled in their groups of friends. I made attempts to be friendly and chime in, but I soon realized that my efforts made the other girls angry, and only caused them to dislike me even more.

I was missing the friends I grew up with in my old school, people I had known since I was in kindergarten. Everyone here still seemed to have their kindergarten friends. I was the odd ball.

Because I had no idea how to interact with people, it was easier for me to just stay away from them. I walked alone at recess, even pretending to have fun when others would walk by just so I wouldn't seem like a bored loner. But the humiliation didn't stop. The other kids continued to make fun of the 69 shirt I wore on the first day of school. I still don't remember what they said or what they meant. I didn't even comprehend what was wrong with my shirt for the first several weeks, but I never wore that shirt again. No one bothered to explain it to me for a long time.

The new school was nothing like I had seen on the TV shows. I figured that Mom and Ian had lied to me about how great this was supposed to be. Instead of making friends, I was inside my head all day just trying to understand these people and how everything worked. For weeks, I was afraid to get in line at the cafeteria. I didn't understand how lunchrooms made lunch *for* you. I was used to bringing my lunch box, but I didn't see anyone do that here. At the end of the table, I sat by myself eating a lunch the other kids called gross.

I also didn't understand why we had computer time where we could play games. Plus, I had never seen the clothes that everyone was wearing and didn't understand the cool words they were using. None of it made sense.

My awkward quirks became known to both myself and everyone else. I was the last one picked for teams in gym class and ignored when I opened my mouth. I was exhausted from trying so hard. I just gave up.

But my teacher must have noticed because one day, when I was sitting alone at lunch, she came over to me and asked me to pick up my tray and to follow her. She led me to another part of the lunchroom where another girl was sitting alone too.

"This is Beth!" Mrs. Crum said. "Beth this is Monica. You guys have to learn three things about each other by the time lunch is over, okay?" She then walked away, leaving us by ourselves.

I stood for a moment, confused and nervous, staring at the girl. I sat down, awkwardly smiled and began to make conversation. It was the last thing I wanted to do, but I felt stuck, and it only took a few minutes for me to see that we had nothing in common. Absolutely nothing.

Our conversation was staggered and dull. The time together seemed filled with silence. It was almost as if we were eating lunch alone anyway. Beth was a tomboy who enjoyed sports, which I had zero interest in. She liked strange animals that I had never heard of or thought were scary. She liked the subjects I was worst at. I wanted to go back to my quiet spot at my original table and be alone. Now, I was dreading lunch time just as much as math time.

Every day I went home with homework on top of the work I didn't finish in class. I couldn't comprehend any of the subjects other than Spelling. For most of the day, I put my head down and prayed the teacher wouldn't call on me.

Being at home granted little relief from school. I would ask Mom to help me with homework, but she always hesitated at that question. She would try to sit with me and help, but after a few moments she couldn't understand any of it either. Sometimes she would try to show me a way I had never seen before. That confused me even more. I wanted to cry. She must have known she couldn't help me because she would call my Tia, who then put my cousin on the phone.

It's useless, I thought. I hated the school and hated the work. I wasn't enjoying it like I had enjoyed my old school. My classmates were cruel and, worst of all, I still didn't have a single friend.

One lonely day at recess I was walking around the playground and saw two girls playing together. One of them appeared to be making up her own game because none of her moves looked familiar. It seemed interesting, so I slowly approached them and asked if I could join.

"Yeah!" she exclaimed, to my surprise. "It's just like this! And then, like this!" Jumping around, she was strangely very happy. I was stunned at her acceptance and didn't even know how to join her. I had never made it past the asking. This was a first for me, and I didn't understand her at all. But then again, I didn't understand anyone else either, so I forced myself to do the hops and jumps she was doing. She was dancing to her own made-up game, and I became a part of it.

Every recess that followed thereafter, I would find Nikki and we would dance this made up game and laugh till our bellies hurt. Looking for her at recess made my days a little happier.

Because school had entangled all of my mental energy and I was trying to decipher this new world of 5th grade public school with millions of social rules, I didn't notice what was happening at home. To my surprise, there was nothing happening, nothing at all.

I was so busy trying to get used to the new home and the new school that I never realized the hostile and futile environment I had lived in on Mozart was suddenly gone. There were no fights, no arguments, no screaming, no yelling, no throwing, no swearing, no hitting and no fear to feel. None. I wondered where it had all gone.

...

Fall 2003

It all began to make sense when Mom, Caleb, Ian and I drove to the downtown Chicago Correctional Facility. We got out of the car and all took turns hugging and kissing Ian good bye. Mom latched her arms around him last and for much longer than I did. When she pulled away, they both stared deeply at one another, each with tears in their eyes. They kissed with passion, and when he slowly pulled away, he kissed her hand and walked towards the building behind him.

Caleb and I got into the back seat and Mom drove off in silence. I knew she was still crying by the sound of her sniffles and the tears that were rolling down her cheeks. She broke the silence and told us that we wouldn't see Papi again for a long time and things would be different now. He would be gone for the next four years, and I couldn't imagine what such a world would look like without him.

...

Terra Haute

WEEKS CONTINUED TO PASS with few words being said. It's possible Mom was sustaining the idea that Caleb and I didn't really understand what had happened. There were many words and conversations that were never had. Though no words were spoken, there was an understanding in the silence.

Eventually, the unfamiliarity of Ian's absence started to fade and familiarity with the new began to take shape. His lingering tension was cycled out of the old air, allowing fresh air to cycle in. Caleb, Mom and I settled into the "it's just us" mentality.

When we had moved to Cedar Forest, Junior had long been absent from our lives, mainly due to Ian's futile relationship with him. Also because Junior had been kicked out of my father's house for stealing. At one point, Junior didn't seem to respect anyone he lived with. Anyone who took Junior in needed a Saint's strength of patience, and he knew that.

Nonetheless, Mom loved him unconditionally and decided he would live with us. He moved in within weeks of Ian's absence. With each visit to the prison before we saw Ian, Mom would remind us, "...and don't say anything about Junior." It was second nature to keep secrets from him; there was always something that had to be hidden.

Our home on Mozart was saturated with terrible memories. Every awful incident of that home was like a torturous flashback to the life we had lived with Ian. Here in Cedar Forest, it felt like a new start.

This home, though distastefully resembling a barn, was cozy inside after Mom and Ian rushed to paint all the rooms, hang new curtains and buy new furniture. It was fresh with our personality. A place for new, better memories that would somehow wash the old ones away. We all had hoped being on this new path meant the old path would be left behind. This was a chance to do things right. Yet, the only problem I saw was that we began the new start without him.

During those weeks, Caleb and I woke up for school and followed our regular routine. We'd get dressed, gather our backpacks and when ready, sit in the kitchen having a quick breakfast together. When there was no time to sit around, we'd heat up our sausage biscuits and snatch them out the microwave with just enough time to make it to the bus.

Mom would arrive home in the morning shortly after we left, and she would fix Junior breakfast. She cooked before he woke and left it covered in plastic wrap on the counter for him. She would roam the house and tidy what needed to be tidied, like our beds that were a mess from our night's sleep or clothes that covered our floor.

But when she was extremely tired from her overnight

shift, she went straight to bed. There was no cooking nor cleaning. Even talking to her was not an option. If she still had some energy, she ran out to do some errands and would make sure to return with enough time for a quick nap before going back to work that night. Naps made it possible to do what she did. But, no matter how tired she felt, she would be the first car in my school pickup line. Over the years, our routine changed a bit, but she was always there, always first.

The weeks flew by this way: first school, then home, followed by homework, dinner, and bed. And then, repeat. Normalcy was filling our time. The only confrontation was between Caleb and me where I would be yelling at him to "go away!" or "leave me alone!" There were also the conversations between Mom and Junior with Junior's never-ending, stressful "Can I borrow your car, Mom? Please! Please! Can I borrow your car?" Junior's relentless badgering to use her white, Pontiac GT was a harassment that happened almost every week.

Sundays were different. Mom would either successfully drag us out of bed or give up and go to church without us. I always felt bad when she did. On the days we fathomed the energy to get up at 9:00 AM, we would attend service at Our Saviors Lutheran Church. It was a church recommended to Mom by a friend from her work, and it had a reputation for having a casual approach to religion.

Caleb and I sat in pews with Mom in just about the same section every service. Some days we'd complain the entire hour, other days' we would doodle quietly or be abnormally giggly. When that happened, Mom separated us by sitting in between us.

After church, the three of us would roam the nearby mall

and pick up large Chillers from our beloved, Gloria Jean Cafe. Caleb and I caught onto this ritual and started attending church just for the mere sugary, frozen treat.

With us in the spotlight of our own lives, I was happier. Yet, something I hadn't thought of was still hovering over Mom's heart. Ian was in prison and would be for the next couple of years. Although I never viewed him as her husband, he was, and I could tell Mom missed him by the sad music she played for months thereafter.

Her sadness and stress grew as her role of being the sole provider for three children settled in. It was a hardship that none of us could relieve. With accumulating bills, school expenses, and unavoidable, unpredictable costs, the financial change was one we all had a difficult time adjusting to.

We all began to change. I was young and understood nothing about true responsibility, nothing about financial priorities, nothing about having people depend upon you. I only knew about fun and the important image I wanted to present at school. I knew there were things I wanted, and she was the one to give them to me. I made nothing easy for her.

Knowing no bounds, I asked for everything and anything I wanted. I hadn't adjusted to our financial change; in my eyes I saw no financial change. With each request for money, I was reminding her of how little we actually had. When she continued to tell me, "No" at my every request and explain, "I don't have any money," I began to resent her.

Selfish and frustrated, one night I questioned her about my father's support check. *How much is it? Where is it going? Why don't I see any of that money?* Although I was aware I was pushing myself to the limit, I didn't care. I spoke like a truly ignorant child and wanted everything.

"That money should be going to me!" I shouted. "I never see any of it. You're not even spending it on me. You spend it on yourself!"

Mom was baffled, but remained silent, laughing under her breath at my obscene rant. She simply let me vent and argue alone. When I saw that she wasn't fazed, I continued to push her, demanding that she answer my twelve-year-old self. But when I realized that she wasn't going to budge and I would get nowhere, I eventually left it unsettled.

The next day, my tias and cousins came to celebrate Thanksgiving at our home. Mom decided to casually bring up the argument we had the night before. She told the family about how I had badgered her and demanded my father's money; how I neglected all of her hard-working efforts as she struggled to simply put a room over our heads and put food on the table. Their eyes widened as they glared at me in shock.

My family responded with, "Monica, you can't do that to your Mom. She's going through a lot." And "Yea, Monica your Mom needs your help right now. She's working hard for you guys." Even, "Monica, you can't be so selfish."

It was then I learned that family is great for blunt honesty and for the next hour, they let me have it pretty well. They had many remarks that made me feel incredibly embarrassed and ugly for the things I had said. They didn't stop either. They wanted to make sure that I really got the point.

So I learned how a family can be a powerful motivator in this way. If you're lucky, you'll have a family who will never sugar coat the things strangers in the real world are going to throw in your face anyway. It is better to hear it first from people you know and trust than from people in the world you don't.

When they were done filling me with guilt, I left the table and stayed alone in my room. I contemplated why I was made to feel wrong and I didn't understand. *Wasn't I right?* I thought. It wasn't fair that I couldn't have any of the things I wanted. After all, it was a check to support me, right? As I debated alone, vocalizing each side out loud, I started to hear my own selfishness. I saw that I had made Mom feel like she wasn't doing enough when, truly, she was doing her best. It was then I knew I was wrong for what I said.

I stopped asking for anything at all. I began to pay more attention to how many burdens she was actually carrying. I wanted to make it up to her and be someone who took her stress away, not someone who added to it. I went to the completely opposite side and began to dread asking for money at all. I avoided it at all costs.

When school made it mandatory to have money for fundraisers, school t-shirts, field trips, or whatever, I didn't bother to bring any of it to Mom's attention. I decided anything that required money meant I couldn't be involved, and I believed Mom when she said she didn't have any money to spend.

I had to accept our limits and decided I would be gentle on Mom's wallet. She was working back to back shifts to make ends meet. The Hollister jeans and Abercrombie shirts that everyone was wearing was not something I could be a part of. That just wasn't going to be me and I had to accept that. We weren't rich, we were barely scraping by. I had to get that through my skull.

Soon enough, I no longer needed reminding. I gave up the image I thought I needed to have. I was trying to figure myself out and grow into the type of adolescent I wanted to be. But I also realized that regardless of what I wanted, Mom's limitations were going to determine that.

Ian wasn't home, but he was still very much involved in our lives; or rather, we were still very much a part of his life. He called us often and Mom sent him money. They arranged visits to see him every couple of months.

He was kept at Indiana's Correctional facility, Terra Haute, which was a three-and-a-half-hour drive from our home in Cedar Forest. It was a drive Mom was not going to take alone due to her fear of driving in unfamiliar places. When she would take a wrong turn and get lost on an unfamiliar road, she would become highly anxious and demanded complete silence. She would roll up the windows, turn off the radio and blast the a/c telling us both to, "Be quiet!" It was a time before GPS.

In order to get her up there, Ian told Mom about a Spanish lady and her two children who lived just a couple blocks from where we lived. Their father was an inmate at the same facility, so Ian and Mom arranged the trip with her. We were to meet her at an outrageous 4:00 AM so that we could drive up for the visitation.

I woke up at an uncomfortable 3:00 AM, disturbed and struggling just to get my body up and to stand long enough to brush my teeth. I had no interest to drive three hours with complete strangers or to see a man who had hurt us. I packed my CD collection, my CD player, and my headphones as well as my drawing tools, paper and a blanket. Mom was ready by the time she woke us up, having woken up much earlier than us. I sat in the living room waiting for her to get Caleb out of bed and was still trying to get my eyes to stay open.

Slowly, we managed to get into her car. The cold of the leather forced me awake along with the chill of the freezing morning air. The garage door seemed so loud in the silence of the morning.

We drove a couple blocks down through the pitch-black neighborhood and arrived at the Spanish lady's street. Mom slowly scanned the homes, searching for the house number. We stopped at what she believed was the place, but there was no indication anyone was waiting for us. After Mom called the woman, she came outside waving us down.

"There she is. Okay, let's go."

We gathered our things from the car and got into the woman's large brown van. Caleb and I sat in the back seats with the woman's children sitting in front of us. Caleb and I had no desire in conversing at such an early hour and even less interest as they appeared to be younger than we were. Mom sat in the passenger seat as the woman started off on our trip to Indiana. As we settled onto the road, I put my headphones on and fell right back into my sleep. The moon and stars still glowing in the sky.

A couple of hours later, the warmth of the sun woke me from my sleep. Caleb sat next to me smiling, patiently waiting for me to wake up. I played through my entire Hawthorne Heights album twice and switched into my Saosin one. I kept to myself for the entire ride listening to the lyrics of my music. I was not feeling any particular way about the visit we were about to have with Ian. It was easier not to care, so I simply flowed with the whole process. I was not resisting or making waves, but just going along with the situation I was forced into anyway. It was going to be the first time we had seen him since he left. I didn't know how to feel about it, so I decided to feel nothing.

As I looked out the window, I saw nothing but empty fields for miles. There were no homes or buildings, nor any sign of civilization. I threw myself back into my music and tried to rest.

Moments later, we turned right onto a long empty road that led to a large building surrounded in sharp, coiled wires. This must be it.

The Spanish lady parked in the large lot and we stumbled out of the van, regaining the feeling in our legs and stretching out the cramps in our bodies.

When we passed through the wide glass doors of the entrance, we were met by security and asked to empty our belongings. Everything and everyone was very, very serious. The walls were gray and lifeless. The staff wore dark clothing and none of them were smiling. The lack of color and light in the building created a silent, confined atmosphere. The only sound was the jingle of security keys and the chatter from the guards' radios. The quiet staff conversations made you feel as if you were in trouble, not a guest who had come to visit.

After making it through the entrance, we were led to a large waiting room with plastic chairs where other small family groups waited. We sat away from the driver and her children and said nothing to them until it was time for us to leave.

Security was taking people in groups up to the visitation floor. We sat anxiously for what seemed like forever. As we waited, I observed the variety of people who were sitting quietly around me. They appeared to be in hopeful spirits and trying to make light out of being here. Many kept their head down and only offered a slight forced smile if they caught my eye. Some remained expressionless. I noticed there were many women and children, just like us.

In the air, I sensed a feeling of shame and embarrassment. As I looked around, I realized that they, too, were waiting to visit an inmate. It was the only reason to be there: to see someone who must have done something horrible, terrible, evil, corrupt, immoral or unforgiving.

After forty to fifty minutes, it was finally our turn. We stood up with other people who had been waiting just as long or longer. The three of us walked to a large metal door and stood still until the guard gave us clearance to pass.

We went through an entrance that led to an empty tan room with silver elevator doors. There was not a single piece of furniture in the room or a picture on the wall. Caleb and I kept close to Mom as she directed us when to move or to wait.

Minutes later, we entered the elevator, along with many of the other visitors. The guard herded us all in like cattle, attempting to squeeze as many as possible into the small space. Once filled to the brim, they closed the doors and took us up.

There were many Hispanic and black women and children sharing the confined space. The distance everyone tried to maintain in the waiting room was replaced by a total lack of personal space in the tight quarters of the elevator walls. Everyone kept silent as the elevator swiftly passed through the floors, and anxiety built the higher we went.

The elevator came to a stop and everyone stepped out

into a large room filled with dark green plastic chairs. The seats were connected, making one large row. We waited in line to be checked in by another security guard who sat behind a tall, solid gray desk that I wasn't able to see over.

As we looked out into the room, we saw families being reunited with their husbands and sons, exchanging bursts of strong affection and joy.

Scanning through the crowds and crowds of people, my eyes stopped on a familiar face.

There he was.

He was standing tall in a gray jumpsuit and his eyes lit up when he spotted us. As soon as we made it through check in, we rushed to greet him, and unexpected tears filled my eyes. He hugged Caleb and me tightly within his arms, and the rough hairs of his moustache brushed our cheeks with his kisses. I stepped aside and watched him passionately embrace Mom. Caleb and I sat down, both looking at one another with disgust as he kissed her with such force. They sat down and we huddled the chairs close together so that we could sit across from him. He held Mom's hands tightly and, with glistening eyes, looked proudly at all of us.

We began talking. It felt so unfamiliar. I couldn't recall the last time we had sat together and enjoyed a simple conversation that didn't consist of rising tension, fear and eventually mayhem. Since I didn't know how this was supposed to go, we tried to relieve the awkwardness by talking about school, grades, Rusty, the house, and anything else that came to our mind.

We told him about the changes that had been happening in our lives over the past couple of months. We told him of the new things we had been doing, the friends we had made and the topics we had been learning in school. We exchanged stories about good, bad, sad and funny times that had happened since he left.

Then he told us about his months in prison. We found out he was a chef in the kitchen, and he told us about his encounters with some of the other inmates. He made it clear to them that he was not someone to be messed with. During his storytelling, he said he told one of the other inmates to stay away from him or he'd regret it. Mom smiled and playfully swatted his leg, "You did not!"

As Ian and Mom's conversation took over about bills and adult matters, Caleb and I asked for the quarters Mom brought. She handed us a heavy change purse that Caleb and I split between us. We took our attention to the vending machines and soon had our hands filled with cheap food. We held up the microwave line, placing each Hot Pocket or White Castle burger in one by one and eventually returning with hot hands. Together, we feasted on the microwavable pizza, burgers, popcorn, chips and soda, as if having dinner at a restaurant, a very strange restaurant.

As we chomped away, they spoke in Spanish about matters they didn't want us to know about. Three to four hours later, when we were relaxed and our bellies full, the guards started announcing departure times. Little by little the crowds that surrounded us slowly dispersed. The seats became empty and the room grew quieter. We slowly started working up to saying a goodbye.

At the last call, we all stood up, and he hugged us even tighter than when we arrived.

"Love you."

"Love you too." I replied. Tears started to stir again.

He hugged Mom last, kissing her the same intense way as when she first arrived. They exchanged words in Spanish, and she tightly squeezed his hand as we slowly trailed off. Standing in the back of the line waiting for the elevator, we watched as the guards lined up the inmates, taking them back by groups.

"Bye," we said, waving sadly. Mom's tears were falling onto her blouse. The guards called him back and he waved goodbye once more, blowing kisses before the door closed. Who knew how long it would be before we saw him again? I instantly began to miss him after he vanished from my sight.

We stood in line silently as Mom wiped away her smeared makeup. We got into the packed elevator, where people were now conversing and making light laughter. There was an entirely different feeling in everyone than on the way up. It seemed as if so much had changed with everyone in those few short hours.

We arrived at the van, the Spanish lady and her children already waiting. I climbed back into my seat and tried to understand the moment, uncertain of what to make of it. I could not figure out my feelings and felt guilty for having any emotion for him at all. Was there something wrong with me for caring about him? I did love him. And I would miss him. Why?

With all her heart, Mom was hoping and praying the next four years would change Ian. She hoped that he would have time to think about the distress, the damage, and the fear that he had brought to this family for so many years. Caleb and I were behind her. We all had hopes he would change into a different man and leave his old ways behind for good. With the many visits we made in the following months, I came to believe that maybe it was possible. I was hoping that we would have a fresh start when he came home.

In the hours we would visit him in his grey jumpsuit, he seemed to be different. He was considerate, thoughtful, and always intently listened to Caleb and me. He showed genuine interest and excitement in the stories of our lives, and expressed love and admiration for all of us through his words and strong, affectionate hugs. His tenderness towards Mom was reflected in the gentle way he talked and held her hands, admiring her eyes during their entire conversation.

All the feelings of anger, of fear, of terror, of control were gone. None of it existed here. All the feelings of tension which had dominated and consumed our lives before were no longer present. It seemed strange. I reflected on my own feelings and where I stood with them at that moment. I noticed I felt closer, like a normal family where love finally existed. We were reconnecting and were better together now. Something about it felt good, really good.

Something about it gave hope.

...

The life of any teenager is a little more complicated than some adults can remember. Life during this time is intense: the feelings, the thoughts, the people, all of it. And realistically, that is the way it should be.

For many, it is during this time when you experience a

lot of firsts: a first best friend, a first argument, a first betrayal, a first love, a first heart ache, a first everything. Whatever the experience may be, it's probably the first one you've had of its kind. It's likely the first time you are actually aware of all aspects to the situation and can make a reasonably informed decision about how you want to behave before, during, and after it.

When Mom and I argued about the car rides she wouldn't give me, the boyfriend I didn't really love, the friend who was a bad influence on me, the clothes I couldn't wear, I grew increasingly furious with her. I started to blame her for the situation we were in. It was because of her, I believed, that we couldn't do the things we wanted to do.

As a know-it-all teenager, I grew to resent her, believing that if she only did what I said, it would solve all my problems. I knew she was a single mother with mountains of responsibility, but I didn't know the depths of her struggles like I do today. With the recurring arguments, I began to look for someone who could help me. I tried looking for someone who would be on my side and try to make her understand that she needed to give me what I wanted. I was truly a self-centered teenager. It was my ugly phase.

Mom wasn't accepting my attitude. "*Aye Dios mio, dame paciencia!*" she would say under her breath as she attempted to hold back what was really on her mind. As I pushed all her buttons and insulted her efforts, she grew furious with me. She looked for help, too.

During her phone calls with Ian, she would hand the phone to me so that he could try to strike some sense in me. But something was different. He didn't yell at me. He didn't grow angry. He only kindly told me, "Hey, I know it's not easy, but you need to listen to your Mom and help her out when she needs it."

"But I just feel like she makes me do the things she's too lazy to do," I snapped and waited for his response. He paused longer than expected, baffled by my words as he struggled to find his own.

"I don't know what to say," he replied. He was at a loss for words, and I was shocked to have made him so.

Ian and I talked more and more over the phone. He showed genuine concern for me and my feelings. He didn't dismiss them; he listened and provided me only with useful feedback. When our conversations were over, I said *goodbye, love you* and handed Mom back her cell phone. She didn't seem pleased at all with how our conversations went.

She may have thought Ian was going to put me in check as he did before. Perhaps he would yell at me, threaten me, or even make me cry. She wanted something from him to whip me into shape. But he did none of that and this was a surprise to both of us. Instead, Ian and I had a conversation. And for the first time, I felt like he was a cheerleader in my corner, even more than Mom had been.

With just about every phone call Mom received, I was to talk with Ian as well. He and I caught up on how I was doing, how Mom and I were doing, and what she and I could work on. He continued to provide me with advice, not forceful orders. He always listened, and never talked over me or raised his voice. He always assured me that everything would be better when he returned. He assured me that all of my stress, anger, frustrations and resentment would be resolved as soon as he came home. He acknowledged that the confrontation in the home was because of his absence, and that he would make things right when he returned. I couldn't wait. Because of our growing relationship, I was excited for his return. I missed him and just wanted him home.

. . .

I graduated from eighth grade in 2006. All during the summer I dreaded what high school would be like. I did what any teenage girl tries to do when something new is approaching; I tried to re-vamp my image. I wanted to be cool. I told myself what I would wear, what I would say. I had to change everything about myself if I wanted to stand out.

Around this time, I grew strongly in love with alternative punk rock music. I got lost in the melodies and my emotions. Caleb and I fell in love with a lot of the same bands which made it easier to ask Mom for T-shirts, concert tickets and other fun merchandise.

My Chemical Romance was my number one. Their dark, intense rhythms spoke to me and all the millions of feelings I couldn't verbalize at the time, some I didn't even know I had until their words sang them out.

Inside, I was angry and depressed about everything. I hated the situation I was in, hated having only one parent around, and hardly ever around when I needed her. I resented Mom for her absence, even though I knew why it was so. That internal conflict was a daily battle. I felt like there was no one for me to talk to and no one even asked. I hated all the limitations I had and resented my peers for their freedom. The only thing that gave me hope was Ian's assurance that things would be better when he came back.

All those emotions eventually spilled out my freshman year of high school. I started the year in Hollister and Abercrombie jeans, but ended the year in Hot Topic punk rock tees, black hair, purple converse and skull jewelry. It felt right. I didn't want to pretend I was something I wasn't anymore. I decided that I was going to be myself and that meant wearing and doing things that other people would surely ridicule me for. I decided I would handle it if it happened, but that being true to myself mattered more. I was not happy, so why pretend to be?

Every night before school, I picked out my outfit for the next day because trying to decide in the morning was impossible and always resulted in my being late. As I looked through my clothes, I paused on the first and only MCR shirt I had. I pulled it off the hanger and sat on my bed staring at the gruesome bloody image of two lovers on the shirt trying to talk myself up. *I'm going to wear it and I won't care what anyone has to say about it.*

I sat the black shirt on my dresser with a pair of jeans and purple converse. It was still brand new; I had only ever worn it at home when I was rocking out to their music videos. I went to bed and convinced myself that I had to start being true to myself now, or I would never be.

At school the next morning, I kept my shirt covered long enough to get to my locker where I finally had to remove my jacket to reveal the bloody couple. I walked with my books to my choir class and sat in my regular seat. It was then, everyone began whispering to one another. Only one other girl said anything. "I love that band!" she exclaimed. I hoped she was being honest.

"Thanks! Me too," I said simply, trying not to make it seem like the big deal I had imagined it to be. In my heart what she said was a big deal. It was the first time I went towards being the authentic me and letting go of any opinions others might have.

After that, the same girl who complimented my shirt wore a pretty unusual band tee herself just a couple days later. Her usual outfits consisted of Hollister, too. I felt relieved to finally stop caring about what other people thought at all. I was going to stop the bullshit, stop trying to fit in and just be myself, however that looked.

I didn't want to care anymore about trying to impress others or trying to be a part of the popular cliques. I was tired of badgering Mom for fifty-dollar jeans and hoodies just so I could uphold an image I so desperately wanted to be a part of. After I began to think about it, it all started to seem so pointless because it wasn't what I wanted anyway. It wasn't me to begin with.

It was the greatest decision I ever made for myself and the best sense of peace resided in me after I decided to just be me.

...

The tumbleweed of emotions I had during the last year of Ian's imprisonment seemed to disperse after I let myself be real. Caleb, Mom and I somehow grew closer together through it all. My passion for MCR allowed us to spend time together in ways we never had.

In March of 2007, we went to downtown Chicago to see

MCR perform the Black Parade live. For the first time, Mom showed interest in our music and became really involved in organizing the whole day. One of her friends from work had a daughter who loved MCR too, so she and Mom made plans for all of us to go together, even taking a limo to get there. I was surprised. Shocked even. *She wanted to go and even arranged a limo to take us? Whoa.*

Needless to say, I couldn't stop thinking about the concert day. I was so excited I kept a countdown for nine months.

When the day finally arrived, I put on all my favorite MCR gear and waited patiently at the front door. Everyone had arrived at our house but, of course, something went wrong. The limo was extremely late by about 30-40 minutes and my entitled, selfish teenage girl came out again.

"Where is it?" I asked Mom every few minutes.

"They said they are on their way," Mom replied calmly.

In another ten minutes, I would ask again. "Mom, are they coming or not?" I grew increasingly irritable and agitated.

After her multiple calls back and forth with the company, they finally arrived at the driveway. I darted inside the van, not a limo, but a van and made it known that we needed to leave NOW! Of course, I deflated Mom's efforts again and made a snarky comment that we didn't even have a limo, but a "luxury van" as the driver said. I didn't care what excuse the driver had for being late or for delivering a van instead of a limousine, I just wanted to get to the concert. My sense of entitlement made me feel like one of the most important days of my life was being ruined. I was fifteen years old and the world obviously revolved around me.

We arrived at the ticket line where blaring loud music

made it impossible to hear one another. The music was unfamiliar. We were early, and only the opening bands were on stage. I was relieved. I followed Mom and her friend to our seats up on the second floor balcony. We had a great view, but I wanted to be right in the very front when they performed, so Caleb and I went to the general standing area and veered our way as close as possible to the front stage.

The lights dimmed, the guitar struck, and the crowd started going wild. It was finally time. The curtains were drawn, and the first opening song was "The End". The intro is slow and acoustic for a minute and then leads up to an anthem of cheers and shouts, with a fast up-beat guitar leading the rhythm. It was the perfect song to get the crowd going.

At the drop where the song changes into mayhem, the curtains flung open, the lights were blaring, and the band started jamming away. I could feel the adrenaline pumping as my eyes gazed on the people who had written the songs that I cherished so much. The crowd was going crazy. There were larger and taller people who were surrounding me, stepping on me, and smashing against me. People soared above my head surfing away on top of the crowd and for a moment, I lost Caleb in all the mayhem.

As the songs kept flowing and the sweaty crowd became even crazier, I somehow managed to grab ahold of Caleb again, but couldn't keep him for long. People kept shoving their way between us, and I could feel him slipping from my grasp.

He started shouting, "I can't breathe! Monica, I can't breathe!" He yelled as the people spilled in between us, pushing him away from me.

I became alarmed, "He can't breathe! He can't breathe!" I

yelled louder and louder.

The people surrounding us began shouting instantly, "He can't breathe! He can't breathe!" More and more started yelling trying to get the attention of the rugged crowd.

"Clear a path!" someone shouted, "Move! Move!"

"Out of the way!" yelled another.

They cleared quickly, letting me back to Caleb and move him out of the mosh. We caught our breath in the open air.

"Are you okay?" I yelled at him, barely able to hear my own words over the deafening music.

"Yeah, yeah, I just couldn't breathe for a second," he said, still trying to steady his trembling.

We decided we couldn't handle the wild crowd and wouldn't make it to the front of the stage like we'd hoped. We went back to the upper balcony to get a good view and just enjoy the show. I called Mom as I walked up the grand cathedral staircase, passing a couple drunk people on the steps.

"Where are you?" I asked.

"I'm with Stella. We're at the bar by the stage," she yelled.

That's awesome! I thought. "Okay, well we're going to stay on the balcony. We'll meet you when the shows over."

"Okay!" she said and hung up.

Did I miss something? She seems awfully calm and cool; she must be having a good time.

Caleb and I finished out the show with a great view. We screamed at the top of our lungs during the final drum solo. The band gave their thanks while the screaming of the fans drowned out their voices. They launched open water bottles into the crowd, and the drummer threw his sticks high out into the air. I watched as people battled for their souvenirs. The band gave their final goodbye and walked off the stage, the red velvet curtains drawing to a close behind them. It was over.

Caleb and I rushed to the front lobby with incredible energy. We were so ecstatic, we lost track of where we were going. We scrambled into the lobby and found Mom with her friend and her daughter. We all piled back into the van. I was so exhausted from the rush I fell asleep on the car ride home. What had first seemed like a ruined day turned out to be one of the best memories ever made possible by Mom.

...

Caleb, Mom and I talked about the concert for days after it had passed and relived it as we listened to the album now more than ever. We all agreed that we had such an amazing time we would have to do it again.

Mom showed me she wasn't kidding either. About a week or two later, I found out that MCR would be returning to Chicago in a few months. I asked Mom if we could go back and see them, and to my surprise, Mom said yes. She said she enjoyed the concert so much the first time that it would be fun to do it again.

There are moments when you're young and your parents, out of nowhere, do something really cool that takes you by complete surprise. This was one of those moments. I looked at her like she was my own rock star.

Days later, she bought the tickets and we were set to see them again. In the days that followed, almost every car ride consisted of an MCR jam session. The only songs Mom didn't like were the ones that had swearing in them, which was only one.

We told Ian about our adventures and he didn't seem to care much for our excitement. "Why are you taking them again?" he later questioned Mom over the phone.

"Because it was fun," was her obvious reply.

"You just went. Now you are going again?" His tone said he didn't like any of it.

"Well, the kids had a good time."

And we did. So much so that we began to do more and more things like this together. Mom began taking us to the movies more often, taking us out to dinner and to pool parties at her friends' homes. The amount of us time had dramatically soared, as well as the amount of her time.

Mom spent more time having fun. She went out with her friends and had girls' night out. They even planned to all get dressed up and meet for the movie premiere of *Sex in the City*. This was her favorite show, next to *Nip Tuck*. That night she got dolled up in her pink shirt, black blazer and brown lipstick. She even took me, Caleb and my friend with her so we could watch a different movie. It was a win-win.

She was having her hair and nails done more frequently; she even took up tanning. She kept a sun kissed glow in the midst of winter and rocked heels all year long. She started dressing a little differently and even asked me to put together some outfits for her.

On top of her shifting self-image, her personality followed right along. She was more vocal, assertive, and direct. She was a little wittier and sarcastic, interested, adventurous and extroverted. I could feel her easygoing tone and spirit growing free. She was transforming and everyone saw it.

All the years of tension had subsided within her. She ventured off in a beautiful way. For the first time, I saw her enjoying herself. These were her years.

As she continued to explore her newfound freedom, her slow growing change mixed with Ian's absence brought us closer together. We argued less and loved more. We disagreed less and laughed more. We were bluntly honest with one another, sometimes hurting each other's feelings, but always turning to one another for help. There was a loving understanding in our new relationship.

It felt like we were in a great place. The depression and anger which initially consumed me seemed to fade away after I let go of the expectations that had been dragging me down.

I let everything go and embraced myself just as I was. Somewhere in the combination of changes, we formed a lasting bond. The love that was never able to be freely expressed was suddenly bursting from the seams. I loved the *us* that we were becoming.

...

At the Correctional Center in downtown Chicago where Ian had been transferred, we made our final visit to see him before his return home. As usual, we were searched by security and waited in the lobby filled with distressed looking mothers and family members. None of it seemed to bother me anymore. Instead, I kept my focus by laughing with Mom and Caleb as we waited.

We took a secure elevator to the visitation floor. It was filled with the same ugly plastic chairs that the last facility had. We took a seat near the vending machines because we knew we would be loading up as soon as Ian sat down.

In our last visits, he had always been waiting and reserving us a spot, but he was nowhere in sight. We waited a few minutes and saw the security guard open the door where the inmates entered. There he was again, but in a different color jumpsuit.

He saw us immediately and greeted us with more love and affection than ever.

Our conversation began and we all took turns helping him catch up on the latest events in our lives. Ian had a surprise for Mom.

"I got a tattoo of you," he said smirking.

"What!'" She laughed and smiled her large smile, "No you didn't."

"Yeah, I did," he continued in his attempt to flirt.

"Really? Where?"

Ian lifted his sleeve and I scanned his arm, waiting to see something. He rolled his sleeve up over his shoulder and there I saw an oversexualized devil cartoon lady. It looked nothing like Mom. "That's not me!" she laughed.

"What? You don't see the resemblance?" He laughed and tapped at my leg.

He then told her about how much he had been working out. He drew his arms out from his sleeve and flexed, showing off his biceps at all angles. Whether she was impressed or not, I couldn't tell, but she didn't say much about it other than smile.

We changed the pace of our conversation and discussed how things would be when he came home. He had some terrible news for us.

Just a month ago, his mother was in an awful accident. She was in her fifties, and as she was driving home from the day's errands, she was hit by a large semi-truck that completely crushed her car. She had been badly injured and suffered permanent damage to her brain and other parts of her body. Her recovery was going to be long, but she would survive. She wouldn't be the same though. Due to her injuries, she would need a caretaker. She would no longer be able to live on her own as she had before. She would need help functioning on a day-to-day basis and couldn't be left unattended. We all listened intently as he made his point.

"So, I was thinking she could live with us," he smiled.

Without a thought, I blurted out, "But where is she going to stay?"

His light smile slowly vanished from his face as he paused at my words and looked into Mom's eyes. It was then I realized I had completely forgotten Junior's living in the house was a secret. I was immediately flooded with guilt, wishing I could shove the words right back into my mouth.

"What does she mean?" he asked. "Did you let Junior back in the house?" His familiar anger grew. I was shocked he already knew who I was talking about.

Mom kept quiet, saying nothing in response.

"After everything I said, you go and bring him back without telling me." His eyes pierced her to her chair. She avoided him and hung her head low.

"He's my son Ian and…"

"I don't care!" he sharply interrupted. "I want him out."

Mom looked up at him, "He's my son. It's my house too."

His eyes widened. They began yelling, much of it in

Spanish. We were surrounded by other families visiting, so I knew he had to control himself. But could he? Caleb and I withdrew, sitting in silence as they argued, gaining the attention of the visitors and guards nearby. She remained quiet and I could see he was pushing her around with his words. All his kindness was gone, and I was looking right back at his old ways.

However, this time he didn't have the same advantage he would have had at home. Normally, in his spirals, he would throw things or raise a hand, but here he could do none of that. And I knew if we were at home, this would turn out much differently.

"Come on, guys," she said, "I don't have to listen to this." Caleb and I immediately stood up. Ian tried to keep her put by standing in her face. They argued for a moment longer, but Mom seemed to decide she had had enough.

She walked away.

We trailed behind her. I watched him as we left. He stood there silent, but the angry look on his face promised we would pay for this later.

The three of us entered the elevator and the doors closed behind us. Mom stood in the corner holding onto the rail, distressed and silent as tears poured down her cheeks. Her sad appearance brought immense guilt to my heart, for I knew this was entirely my fault.

"I'm sorry, Mom," I apologized for the mess I caused.

"It's okay." She smiled looking up at me, tears glossing over her brown eyes, "It's not your fault."

She let out a large sigh, "He hasn't changed."

...

The Second Return

THE CEDAR FOREST BENGALS played almost every Friday night on the school football field. It was homecoming and the second largest event next to Prom. My carefree attitude brought new friends into my life and the dozens of us huddled on the cold metal bleachers to cheer for the players. We were a good mix of guys and girls. The girls and I flirted with the ones we thought were cute and laughed at what I thought were horribly offensive sex jokes. This kind of humor never appealed to me, so when I'd had enough, I actually watched the game that barely anyone else was paying attention to.

I would check in with Mom from time to time; that was the deal. I stepped out of line near the concession stand, while my friends ordered hot chocolate. I called her just to let her know what my plans were for the night.

"Hey, Mom."

"Hey Sweetie, how are you? How's the game?" she asked.

"Good. Umm hey, Nikki asked if I could sleep over tonight

after the game. Can I? Please?" I asked wishfully.

"Mmmm, how are you getting there?" She had been getting better with allowing me time out with my friends, but I could tell she still wasn't going to be an entirely loose parent.

"We have a ride." I said in my attempt to bypass the fact that we didn't. In actuality, we were planning to attend a party some older guys invited us to.

Unconvinced, she asked, "Who's driving you?"

"One of our friends has a car and she said she would take us." I tried again to be convincing.

"Okay, but you call me when you get to Nikki's house. Okay?" she replied.

"Okay!" I said relieved, "I will! Thanks Mom!"

"Okay, be safe." I could hear the concern in her voice.

"I will, I will. Love you!"

"Love you, too."

I went quickly to tell my friend and both of us gushed with excitement.

That night, we went to the party in some twenty-year-old guy's basement. We got tipsy on two beers, flirted a whole lot and played drinking games. This is when I discovered my talent at flippy cup. I went upstairs to my other girlfriend who was making out with some guy and I slid by them to grab a beer from the fridge. It was close to 4:00 AM and I passed out on the couch while listening to people make out in the other rooms.

The next morning as the sun started shining through the thick gray curtains, one of the guys offered to drop off Nikki and me at her house. Nikki's mother had already known where we had been, and she let us in without saying anything.

Nikki and I went back to sleep in her room, still exhausted and smelling of beer. When we woke around noon, her mom ordered Mexican food for us. Nikki and I gossiped about the night and when I was ready, I called Mom to come pick me up.

Mom was a lot more trusting with me after our MCR concerts. She gave me a lot more freedom. It was my first year in high school, so I think she was still getting used to the whole idea. Aside from my better judgment, I took advantage of it when a great opportunity presented itself. Who knew when she would decide to start saying no again?

It made me feel guilty to lie, especially when I could see she was putting forth the effort to trust me. The lying wasn't like me, so I tried to avoid it whenever possible. I even considered she might be right about my bestie being a bad influence on me, but I would never confirm any of that to her.

I respected her much more after the privileges she was beginning to allow me, so I decided that if she said no, it was no. That was okay. She started coming around so much that I began to realize we had an understanding with one another. There was a respect and trust in one another, and it was a trust I didn't want to break.

...

In August 2007, I suggested going to the White Sox game with my friends since my school was offering discounted tickets and a bus ride for all the passengers. She agreed and bought tickets for both herself and Caleb as well. She was becoming much more outgoing than I had ever known her to be.

The day of the game, I met my friends in the school parking lot and after a thirty-minute drive, we arrived at US Cellular Field. It was the first time I had ever watched a baseball game with my Mom. We all hiked to the top of the bleachers where the players looked as small as ants, but the view made the whole experience worthwhile.

My friends and I gawked at the players with the best rear, ate hotdogs, and took tons of photos to post on Myspace. It was everything you would expect for a first-time ball game. Mom even asked me to take pictures of her in her White Sox jersey as she stood in front of the railing, posing with her hands of her hips. I was impressed by her confidence and loved it. It seemed to be a year we were trying new things and stepping into unknown territory with courage.

That same year I decided I would try out for the badminton team. Badminton was the only sport I ever enjoyed. I had considered cheerleading in the past, maybe even dance, but none of them seemed to fit. Since I was still committed to being myself, I went for what I liked.

I told Mom about the tryouts and she gave me the extra encouragement I needed. I reminded her about the games I would have to attend, the gear I would need to buy, the money it would cost, the time it would take. Without any hesitation, she agreed. It made me wonder what had changed in our finances, but I kept my thoughts to myself.

"We'll make it work," was her only reply.

There were no longer questions of prevention, just a loving cooperation. She offered to pick me up after practices and attend my games if she was able to. That boosted my excitement even more.

In the days leading to tryouts, I knew I wasn't anywhere close to being fit, so I chose to attend the spring conditioning which was designed by the school to get students ready for the spring sports. All of my friends had decided to do sports too: soccer, softball, basketball, and volleyball. But I was the only one who had decided to do badminton. *That's fine, be yourself.*

One of my best friends was trying out for softball. During class, she asked me to join her for the first conditioning day of the year. Though I was unprepared and had no clothes to work out in, she agreed to lend me her gym suit in hopes that it would persuade me. It did.

After the last class of the day, I met up with her in the locker rooms, which were flooded with other girls getting ready too. She was changing at her locker while I went to the bathroom stall; never one to change in front of others.

I put on her shirt and shorts and walked back to her locker to put my shoes on. When I lifted my leg to the bench I gasped at how unprepared I really was.

"Uh oh." My heart sank.

"What?" she asked.

"Oh no."

"What! What is it!"

"I, uhhh. I can't do this," I finally responded.

"What!" she exclaimed. "Why!"

"I haven't shaved! At all! All winter!" I tried to be quiet, "Look!"

My legs resembled that of a very hairy man's. They were long, dark and completely unfeminine. Mortified by the mere sight, I immediately backed out of my commitment.

"It's not that bad!" She didn't sound very convincing.

"What? Yes, it is! I can't do this, I'm leaving." I gathered my clothes.

"No! You can't," she yelled, "Who cares? No one's going to be looking anyway." But I didn't believe her.

"No. Nope, nope." I had decided and started getting dressed, "No."

"You have to! C'mon, please! Please do it for me."

"What?" I asked.

"Do it for me, c'mon," she repeated, seemingly disappointed. I paused and looked at her, trying to decide if that was reason enough.

"Please?" I looked around at every girl's perfectly shaved legs and groaned to myself. I felt like I would regret this, but she was right. I had made a commitment to her. I had also made a commitment to myself; I wasn't going to care what other people thought anymore. Period. To my dismay, I felt like that included this, too.

"Uhhhh, ohh alright," I said, losing all motivation.

"Yes!" she shouted with a large smile. "Thank you!"

I pulled the shorts back on and tied my shoes, angry at myself for committing to this at all.

We sat in the hallway and waited for direction from the conditioning coach. When the coach finally arrived, she arranged everyone into six lines. We started out with what I believe was entirely appropriate; butt kicks. When it was my turn, I slowly jogged across the hall, kicking myself in the rear with the heel of my foot, something I was mentally doing anyway. As I felt every hair on my leg blowing in the air, I imagined that this must be how guys feel. Gross.

After a good couple of warm ups, I began to entirely forget about my ladyless legs. I had a goal in mind: I wanted to make the team. So I focused on what really mattered: getting myself into shape. As a result, I plunged through the rest of the straining workouts.

When training was over, I was doused in a sweat of accomplishment. I sped back to the locker room, eager to get home. I was the first in the bathroom stall to be getting dressed. I passed by my friend as I was walking out and smiled at her.

"I'll kill you later."

I attended the next training sessions with smooth, shaved legs. When the training season ended, it was time for badminton tryouts.

I completed the three days of tryouts with flying colors, getting praise from the coaches on my form and my ability to keep pushing through. I told Mom how well it went and we both hoped I did good enough to make the team. The list would be posted the next day, and we were both eager to see if I made the cut.

The next morning, we rushed to school a little ahead of schedule, and she dropped me off at the front of the school doors.

"Okay, you're gonna let me know?" she asked.

"Yeah! I'll give you thumbs up if I made it and thumbs down if I didn't," I responded.

"Okay, good luck!" she said. "Love you!"

"Okay, love you too." I shut the car door, nervous as I speed walked to the front doors and darted my eyes to the list. I scanned the list of names and stopped.

There I was: *Monica Medina - JV Team.*

I turned around and threw my thumbs up in the air, jumping and smiling with excitement. I had made the team! I could see Mom jumping and clapping in the driver seat of her car. She waved with excitement at me and blew a kiss through the open passenger window. Ecstatic, I waved back and blew a kiss her way.

I was filled with pure joy, and I could see she was, too.

...

A week after our last visit with Ian, he called to apologize about his behavior. He validated Mom's rights to the house and her right to parent her son. When I had my turn with him on the phone, he appeared apologetic, explaining that his behavior was inexcusable and he was terribly sorry to have upset us. He asked for something he had never asked for before.

Forgiveness.

It was the first time I felt he was truly being transparent and genuinely sincere. He wasn't being confrontational, threatening or hostile at all, especially over the past couple years we had visited him.

It wasn't until I leaked out some unpleasant news about Junior that his old ways showed themselves. But I didn't fault him. It was obviously my fault. I saw him as a different man. I forgave him. *No one is perfect.*

Change, like anything else, takes time. Sure, it was a hiccup in the road, but I saw it only as a minor setback and was thankful we were able to put it behind us. That's what families do, forgive and move forward. It felt right and we all seemed to veer back on track. We all returned to the happy anticipation of his arrival.

However, as the time came closer, Junior was still living with us and Ian would be returning home in the next couple of months. Given their futile history and clashing personalities, Junior could never live with Ian and Ian could never live with Junior. Mom was being forced into making a decision. Just a few weeks before Ian's release, Junior moved out.

...

Winter 2007

All day long, sitting in class, it was the only thing I could think about. I was boiling in a pot of mixed emotions: excitement, anxiety, hope, confusion and a thousand more conflicting feelings. I was eager to start a life that Ian could be a part of. With all of our newfound personalities, I wondered what shape life would take on now. Our days on Mozart were long behind us. Painful memories and feelings that once came so frequently were now long in the past. We were living in the fresh start we had always wanted.

In the past four years, we had all become different people from the ones who had lived on Mozart. Mom had grown in confidence and independence, Caleb with great humor and loving heart. For me, I was explorative. I still loved my punk rock jams, but as I became happier, I gravitated towards happier lyrics. Through music, I discovered myself. At only fifteen, I found my self-esteem and growing tenacity.

We were entering a new part of our lives with Ian and I knew it would begin as soon as I arrived home from school and opened that door.

"Hello? Mom?" I called as I took off my gloves.

"Hi sweetie, we're up here," Mom replied from the kitchen. I took off my wet boots and laid them next to the door. I walked up the stairs to see Mom and Ian sitting at the kitchen table. My eyes took a moment to process. He was not in a jumpsuit but regular clothing. He was sitting at a table, not in a solid, plastic chair. It appeared entirely surreal. He was here in the kitchen.

At that moment, I realized that I had almost no memories of him ever being in this house. He had left so soon after we moved in and I realized he never had a chance to make this his home.

Something else was different. There was nothing to be wary of. There was no threatening or hostile behavior; no yelling, screaming, or arguing. Yet my body seemed to strongly remember the fear that had once consumed it so intensely. Inside, I tried to block that out.

He smiled a large smile when he saw me and threw his arms open. I embraced it and leapt into him. He squeezed me tightly and though I squeezed him back, I was still trying to make sense of his presence.

"How was your day, sweetie?!" Mom asked.

Staring at Ian, I felt distracted, "It was, uhh, good!" I replied. "I'm gonna go put my things in my room."

Needing time to absorb it all, I walked to my room. I didn't understand why I had felt so strange. I had known for the past four years that Ian would be returning to us. I had been blissfully excited, ecstatic even, waiting for the day he returned. In all the excitement, I never imagined what it would truly feel like when the day came because I didn't see it as a day to prepare for. In my vision, there was nothing but happiness to look forward to. Yet, seeing him in the kitchen made it all too real. My feelings shifted and I sensed something else was about to change as well.

I eventually came back to the kitchen and tried to act as I normally would when I arrived home from school every other day.

"Do you have homework?" Mom asked.

"Oh, yeah I do. I'll get it." I grabbed my homework from my backpack and sat at the dining room table, taking my time with it as they chatted at the table with coffee. That Friday, something seeped into the air.

Later that night, Mom left to work her regular night shift and return in the morning. Caleb and I stayed up in my room, watching television and playing video games on the Nintendo that was passed down to me. Every weekend, we would laugh hysterically while playing Mario Kart, killing the other person with the shells or stars. We also loved Perfect Dark, where we would throw the mines all over each other and see which one of us exploded first. Our laughing banter would continue into the late hours of the night.

Ian remained downstairs, watching television and smoking relentlessly in the living room. His smoking was a habit I hadn't missed. Every time I went to Dad's house, my stepmother, Lydia, would wash all my clothes upon arrival because they reeked of cigarette fumes. My friends never wanted to borrow my clothes and I figured this was why.

Our first evening reunited with Ian was oddly silent and distant until he came up from the basement and told us it was time to go to bed.

"We never go to bed at this time," we said, confused.

"Well, I'm home now and it's time to go to bed," he repeated.

I'm like my mother in many ways. I hate to make waves. In order to avoid conflict, I listened to his direction, even though I disagreed. Caleb on the other hand, didn't agree at all, and spoke out.

"Mom says we can stay up," Caleb retorted.

"Did you hear what I said?" Ian asserted, growing louder with an old familiar tone. "I said it's time to go to bed. You guys have been walking all over her and that ends now." That sudden statement made me think, *just how have we been walking all over her?*

Caleb and Ian argued as they trailed off into the living room. I stayed at my bedroom door watching them. Caleb continued to argue, frustrated that our routine was being broken without reason and against Mom's permission. Ian grew increasingly frustrated. In the midst of Caleb's refusal, Ian suddenly struck him across the face.

I gasped and stood in shock.

Caleb looked back at Ian in surprise with tears beginning to form. I came from my room to comfort him.

"You didn't have to hit him," I said to Ian, taking Caleb back to my room.

. . .

The next morning when Mom arrived home from work, tension immediately welcomed the day.

"What happened?" Mom shrieked. Caleb and I explained

to her about the night before, and Ian immediately seemed to feel threatened.

"You let these kids walk all over you! You let them do whatever they want!" he shouted.

"Your first day out and you do this!" She spoke the words I had been thinking, "My goodness, you haven't changed."

His voice grew stern, "Yes, I have." He grabbed her arm and looked intently into her eyes, but her only response was a look of disappointment. "Hey, listen. I have changed," he pleaded.

"Then what is this?" she exclaimed, yanking her arm free and gesturing at Caleb's face. "You just get out and you're already back to your old ways?" Mom didn't seem to accept any of his justifications. It was the first time I saw her standing up to him. She wasn't allowing an excuse or an 'I'm sorry.' "I can't believe this," she continued, "I thought things were going to be different."

"Hey, things are going to be different," he said. He tried to convince her, but she wasn't the same person who would be so easily swayed. She wasn't the same person he remembered.

"Yeah, okay," she replied, upset and unconvinced.

As I listened to their argument, she spoke freely and didn't hold back or keep it all in, as she had done in the past. I realized she was being strong and holding her own. I was proud of her.

At the same time, my heart ached for Mom because I, too, felt entirely fooled. The past four years seemed like a bold lie fed straight to our faces. I started to reexamine the years we spent without him and regretfully began to think that may have been our opportunity to get out.

Every visit we had spent with him in prison seemed like

nothing more than an act now. He had given us a great theatrical performance. But why? Why go through all the trouble of pretending, faking and lying to us just to come back and be the same angry man? I didn't understand and looked at the adult world with even more confusion.

The next day when I had time alone with Mom, I asked her what she thought of the whole thing and she immediately began to cry. She told me that she thought he had put on a show because he was afraid she would leave. She then said that she had discovered free programs that exist for battered woman to divorce their husbands if they are incarcerated. I was deeply saddened.

"Really?"

"Yeah. I thought about it too," she said.

"Why didn't you?" I questioned her, upset that she hadn't taken advantage of the programs.

"I thought he would change," she sighed. That was the truth. We all thought he would change. She already seemed to regret her decision, so I said nothing more. Even though I now wished she'd chosen differently; I couldn't be upset at her for thinking the same thing we all had. *He was supposed to change.*

My hopes for our life as a family had been deflated all too quickly. I had hoped that the same kind, caring person we experienced during the prison visits would be the same kind, caring person who would come home. Oddly enough, even after Ian revealed himself that night when he hit Caleb, I was still hoping he could somehow be that changed person.

Within the initial weeks of Ian's return, there was much to adjust to. I began to feel the power struggle rising in the home

between him and Mom. Caleb and I had been so used to looking to Mom for everything that we continued to do so, even in
his presence.

In our eyes, she was still the head of the house. She had
been doing everything on her own for the past four years to
earn that respect. I had watched her mow the lawns in the hot
blistering summer, trim the hedges, plant a garden and shovel
the snow in the freezing winters. Every day, she had slept short
naps in the afternoons and woke up at night to work a double
shift.

She had been responsible for all the bills and was still
somehow able to provide Christmas presents as well as host our
birthday parties. On top of it all, she maintained three children
and a dog.

Whether Ian was feeling jealous, resentful or inferior, I
didn't know. But he immediately tried to take back his control
by adding some new rules: no food in the rooms, no clothes on
the floor, no eating past 8:30, no loud music. He was trying to
control us by any means possible. But I had grown so accustomed to Mom's relaxed ways that I couldn't handle his strict
orders and it only created problems.

He didn't like that Mom had a voice now. He also didn't
like Mom's newfound interest in going out with her friends. He
questioned her about where she had been, what she was doing
and who she was with almost every waking minute. When she
would defend herself in reminding him that she was a grown
woman, capable of doing what she pleased, his anger only spiraled.

I took no chances in these moments, for I knew what he
was capable of. I kept close to my phone and called the police

anytime I needed to.

When it was necessary, the police would arrive with lights flashing in our driveway and assess their dispute. Their presence in defusing the situation was only temporary. I was always fearful that Ian's anger would only be triggered once they had left.

Thankfully, he was on probation. That may have deferred him from taking any further action as he normally had in the past. But it was early in his return, and although it was not starting in the way we had hoped for, we tried to move toward happiness and make it work.

...

As I sat at the dining room table one afternoon doing homework, I listened to them laugh and giggle in the basement, something they had never done before. Their laughing grew a little louder and then, instead of laughs, I heard cries. I turned around and saw Ian racing up the stairs with Mom hoisted over his shoulder. She looked lifeless.

I screamed at the sight.

She was hurt, she must be hurt. Did he kill her? Is she alive? In less than a millisecond, my mind sprinted down the whole list of possibilities. I jolted out from my chair and fell to my knees, sobbing uncontrollably on the living room floor.

My shrieking cries surprised them. Ian stopped instantly in his tracks and slowly let Mom down to stand. She looked at me. Her eyes were alarmed and confused.

She was unharmed.

"What is it, sweetie?" Her voice was soft and gentle. What I had thought made it difficult to answer her.

"I... I...." I couldn't say the words. "I thought he killed you! I thought you were dead!" I tried to control myself and was relieved to see I was terribly wrong.

"Oh, honey, no." She tried to calm me, "I'm fine. We're fine. We were just playing."

"I know," I cried hysterically, "but it looked like you were dead." I couldn't believe I had made such a grave mistake.

I recognized that my outburst had ruined their play. I looked up and saw the sheer disappointment on Ian's face as he stood there.

Mom trailed behind him, "She didn't know." She tried to comfort him, but he tossed his hand out and stopped her as he walked away.

He was trying to be the different person he said he was going to be; the different person we had hoped for and I felt guilty for having assumed the worst of him. Thereafter, Ian would always refer to himself as "The Bad Guy."

...

At a rapid pace, Ian began to fall back into the old anger and took us all back with him. He created thick, familiar tension in the air, making it nearly impossible to breathe the oxygen.

In his presence I found myself worried at all hours of the day. I was always nervous that something was about to happen even though all was quiet in the home. It didn't matter what time of day it was, or if it was a holiday or special occasion. It didn't matter if we were all enjoying our time or not, and it didn't matter if I was alone or with someone else. It didn't even matter if Ian seemed to be in a good mood. My nerves began to consume all my mental energy and created a need in me to be aware of what everyone was doing at any given moment. The mental stress kept me safe, or so I believed.

Every time I overheard Mom and Ian talking, I quietly crept to my door and nudged it open. I would listen carefully, trying to determine if an argument was going to be triggered. When I felt confident that all was calm, I eased back from my door and continued with whatever I was doing. It was an involuntary response that became a regular part of my life. I was fearful and had to know if she, or we, were going to be in danger.

During the time that Mom was in the bathroom getting ready for work, everyone crowded into that small space swarming for her attention. With her busy schedule, it was the only time she stood long enough in one place. It seemed to be the best opportunity to talk with her or, in Ian's case, argue with her.

Every night she stood in front of the large mirror in her heels, white bra and black work pants up at her waist while she blow-dried her soft curls and straightened her bangs. She always kept a pink roller in her hair till she walked out the door.

She leaned over the counter to apply her makeup, her mascara never quite making her eyelashes as long as she would like. "Why can't I make mine like yours?" she would ask. Then, she would gently put on her white shirt and finish with her bright red blazer and dash of *Pleasures* perfume.

It was a routine I became quite familiar with because I was usually bothering her from the toilet seat. Other nights, however, I would be in bed. During one of her get-ready routines, I heard Ian walk into the bathroom and begin questioning Mom. I couldn't understand Spanish, but I understood the tone of voice. They argued back and forth, their agitation rising with every retort. As their words intensified, Ian slammed the door shut. I was already at my door listening. A moment later there was a loud crash. I jolted from my room and rushed to the bathroom where I knocked on the door in a panic.

"Mom! Are you okay?" I shouted through the door.

"We're busy!" Ian yelled.

"I need to know if Mom is okay!"

"I'm okay, Sweetie," she said softly in quiet distress.

Ian flung open the door and stormed out past me. I saw Mom turned around at the sink, unharmed, looking at her things scattered on the bathroom floor.

"Are you okay, Mom?" I asked.

She placed her hand to her forehead, "Yeah." She looked at me, smiling, with tears that were already drying, "I'm okay."

. . .

Uncertainty was everywhere. I kept close to my phone when Ian and Mom were home. When I couldn't be available, like when I was taking a shower, I panicked. Taking a shower was normally a time I would enjoy pampering myself and entertaining random thoughts while lathering up good-smelling shampoo. Instead, the tiniest noise made me jump out of my skin, shut the water off and rush to the door only to hear a kitchen cabinet shut, a door slam, or a piece of silverware drop. Every noise triggered a paralyzing fear, leaping my thoughts into the belief something terrible was happening outside the door.

On numerous occasions, when I believed that what I heard was truly a confrontation starting, I would spring out of the shower, dripping water all over the tile floor and throw on a towel. I'd keep huddled behind the bathroom door, listening for a clue.

"Mom?" I would say, and if I heard nothing, again I would say "Mom?" just a little bit louder.

"Yeah, honey!" The sound of her voice immediately calmed me.

"Nothing!" I would try to sound relaxed and close the door quietly. Once relieved that she was unharmed, I mopped up the water and finished my shower, feeling no more relaxed than when I started.

...

February 2008

An obvious divide grew between Ian and me. I tried to avoid him at all costs unless it was absolutely necessary. Although he continued trying to get us together, he had shown me one too many times there was another side to him that could easily strike without warning.

Aiming to keep the peace, I would force a smile; assuring him everything was fine. It felt like acting, and I was no good at acting.

As I grew older, I had less and less motivation to interact with Ian. Having turned sixteen, I was fed up with the whole absurd performance. It was all like a song I had heard way too many times, a movie I had grown sick of, or a shirt I had worn out. I was over the entire happy-daughter-nothings-wrong role. I was finished with the tip-toeing around, the fake smiles, and the constantly repressed honesty about what was really happening, what was really bothering me and what I really wanted to say. I resented my forced smile that said this was all okay. My fake-it tank was running extremely low, but I was thankful Caleb and I continued to keep the same close bond with Mom.

On numerous rides in Mom's car, which was the only time we were alone together, we spoke freely. It gave us time to vent our problems to one another. First, we would wait in the car while Mom picked up her lotto ticket inside the convenience store. When she got back into the car, she would dig through her purse, pull off the cap to a red lipstick, thoroughly apply it to her lips, then kiss the top of her ticket that she hoped would be a winner. After she placed the ticket above her visor, we would then vent about encounters with Ian and the frustration it was causing us.

Caleb and I had no filter. We told Mom exactly how we felt about him with not-so-nice words. In return, she was boldly honest with us.

She explained that she was heartbroken with Ian and that her hopes for a fresh start had been crushed. She revealed that she was tired of being treated like a child, tired of his abuse, tired of his control. She was done trying to keep him happy. She seemed entirely transparent, unleashing all of the emotions and thoughts that seemed to have been cooped up. She cried under her sunglasses and told us that she still loved him, but she knew he hadn't changed. And every time she told us, "He's not going to do this to me anymore," we encouraged her to be strong. We reminded her that she was right and deserved better.

...

Ian's return left all of us struggling in different ways. Junior had moved out, and with nowhere to go, he soon became home-less. He had only his car and a couple bags of clothes. During the following months, while I'd be watching television in my room, my attention would be caught by the pebbles hitting my window. When I checked to see what it was, Junior would be standing down below asking me to open the door for him. He usually never came if anyone was home. I'd open the front door and he'd come in to raid the fridge, catch up with me and Caleb and talk to us about Mom and what she was doing with Ian. Neither of us ever had any answers as to what was happening. When Ian returned from prison, Junior had been forced to leave. His absence caused Mom to build up immense resentment towards Ian for forcing her into such an agonizing place as a mother. Mom pleaded with Ian, trying to convince him to allow Junior to live with us. I felt her distress grow as she was refused every time. Mom soon realized that nothing she said would ever convince Ian otherwise.

When it was possible, Mom would allow Junior to come by the house for a shower, warm food, and money. She would send him off just before Ian arrived back from the day's errands. For the rest of the harsh winter months, we continued in this way without Ian's knowledge.

...

As the end of the school year began to grow closer, summer started to peek around the corner. Mom and Ian were distant, barely speaking and sleeping apart. The tension was silently suffocating me. It was during this time that I began reading a book in my literature class called *The Breakable Vow*.

As the teacher moved through a new chapter each day, I began to realize that the content was strikingly familiar to me. I started walking alongside the main character through her journey of violence and fear and her fight to survive. I related much of her experience to my own as well as to Mom's.

It came as a complete revelation to me to have found a book that discussed such a secretive topic. I was amazed to hear there were nearly identical stories happening to other people. It felt like a switch had turned on all the lights to a room that had long been dark and dormant in my life.

I read forward and discovered what the cycle of violence was: there was the tension-building phase, the battering phase, and the honeymoon phase. There it was. All the pieces of my life put together like a child's puzzle, describing Ian with incredible precision. It was dead on.

Why had I never known this? I sat at my desk with my heart in my stomach, listening to my teacher finally make sense of my entire life's story and answering all the questions that made me believe I was crazy for even thinking them. That teacher was the first person to explain what I had questioned for so long and although I was in a class of twenty-five other students, it seemed like she was speaking directly to me.

Up until that point, I didn't believe this was something anyone could make sense of. If you could, you had magical powers from faraway lands. With my mind opened, I began to replay every memory of tension and battery that was always followed with sweet, apologetic lies.

All my life, I believed I was alone in dealing with this terrible monstrosity. With the limited knowledge I had prior to this class, I had tried to make sense of my life, but never could. At last, I had answers.

I finished the book ahead of schedule and reread the chapters along with my class. Days after we finished the novel, we sat in the lecture hall, greeted by a guest speaker with a personal story to tell on dating violence. My class, as well as others, flooded into the lecture hall searching for a seat. I went straight to the front.

When all were quiet, he began. He told us a story about his daughter and a boy she had met and all the horror that followed. She was a young teenager about my age and was trapped in the same cycle of violence we had just learned about. He became tearful as he spoke about the pain this boy had caused his daughter and how he eventually caused her death.

It was a difficult story to hear, and probably even more difficult to tell. He urged us never to fall victim to such evil and to help others who may be blinded by this illusion of love. By the end of his personal, heart gripping story, I was in tears, but never thought for a single moment Mom's situation would ever go as far as his daughter's.

...

During our free speaking car rides with Mom, she told us about plans and ideas she had, about her feelings and frustrations as well as checking in with us to see how we had been holding up. We would joke, more than anything, and imagine a life without him somewhere on a tropical beach. We were reminded of the freedom his imprisonment had brought us during those four years and how his absence had brought us happiness that we never had before. It was a time when we had a glimpse of a different life, and we wanted it back.

Whenever she mentioned leaving Ian, Caleb and I great-ly encouraged her, reminding her of how strong she was now. We told her she didn't need him anymore and that she would be better off without him. It was a topic that ultimately went nowhere. It was no more than a hope and dream. Imagination kept it alive.

But soon, she began to bring up the topic more than usu-al with more detail than ever before. She began talking about locations, costs, timing, and so on and told us she didn't want to take us out of school. I was about to go into my second year of high school with no desire to leave it, so she agreed to keep us close.

She began telling us about the rules we would need to have if this were to be successful. I didn't notice immediately, but she was prepping us.

1. He couldn't know anything about it. Not a single word. This was crucial. She stressed the importance of not blurting things out again, Monica! I was reminded of the Junior incident and how I had derailed Mom's se-cret. I wouldn't do that again. The hurt it brought Mom had been marked on my heart.

2. We were only to discuss the move when we were alone together. Not in the house. Not via phone, not via text, nothing.

3. Do not start packing. Gathering boxes would only de-rail the whole thing. Instead, Mom said she would start moving things little by little, in order to keep plans as undetected as possible.

4. Do not tell anyone. It would be difficult to keep our own mouths shut, telling anyone would only jeopardize the plan.

In all honesty, I wasn't listening too much during the first few conversations. As much as I wanted to leave, I didn't believe we were really going through with it, so I ignored most of it. At first, I believed the hype would eventually die off and we would just continue to deal with Ian like we had our whole lives. Yet weeks passed and the topic wasn't dying off. The hype wasn't fading. In fact, it became stronger.

Mom eventually snatched my full attention when she started telling us about an apartment she had looked at. "Do you guys want to see it?" she asked. "Junior has already seen it. He said he liked it!"

It finally sank in. *We're really doing this? We're really leaving?* Once I began to believe it, my thoughts overwhelmed me. I hadn't given myself any time to process the change, and my mind spun at the realization that it was possible Ian would no longer be in our lives. This wasn't venting conversation anymore. This wasn't daydreaming or wishful thinking any longer. Mom wasn't leading false hopes. She started organizing.

She started planning.

...

Get Out

Opening the door at the end of the hall, I was welcomed by a small entry space along a white, half wall overlooking the dining area. I entered the brightly lit white kitchen and looked out the balcony near the living room. It was on the third floor with a view out over a parking lot and the main street.

I scoped out the bedrooms, bathroom, and closet space. It was small: two bedrooms and one bathroom. Smaller than what I had been used to, but a sacrifice I wasn't going to complain about since Mom was already taking such a risk. She decided that she and Caleb would share a room while Junior would fluctuate between Mom's bed and the sofa's pullout bed. Thankfully, Mom allowed me my own room.

"What do you guys think?" Mom's face lit up with curiosity.

"I like it!" I truly did. The apartment was tucked at the end of a long hallway in the back of the building and hard to find. That was a positive for us. It was the second place I'd seen, and

I was set on it.

Mom was cautious and started planning with extreme care. We were to move out during the week when Ian was at work. Caleb and I would miss school and begin packing on move-out day.

Mom's friends had long been aware of her situation, and she recruited as many as she could to help us get our things out the door. After she reserved the moving truck, all was set. We waited.

The excitement of the new place was equally matched by my fear of leaving the old one. Carrying this incredible secret made me excessively nervous with the rising anticipation as the day came closer.

Every time I saw Ian, I tried to keep it together. I was afraid I would blurt it out at any moment, so I just tried to avoid conversation all together. *What would he do*, I wondered, *if he knew what we were planning?* I tried to ignore the doubt that told me this could all blow up and go horribly wrong, that this could be either the best or worst decision we had ever made. *Was it even worth trying? Were we making the right choice? Yes!* I yelled at myself. Certainly there must be a better life than a life of fear. My mind told me this was the right thing to do, but my body was shaking at the thought.

I deeply admired Mom. She was finally doing it and I was astonished at her courage. She may have been just as terrified as we were, but she didn't show it, so I tried to find my strength from her. Up until now, Caleb and I had urged her to leave, along with so many friends and family, but to no avail. This time was different. Mom was taking action.

The solution was simple enough. I knew that if we ever

wanted to be happy, this is what it would take. The past had shown us that happiness could never happen if he was around. This was our chance at it.

...

Summer 2008

It was early, but I could no longer sleep. I could hear Mom rustling around in her room. I jolted out of bed and she greeted me with a smile that reassured me, we could do this. Time was limited. I had to start now.

Mom handed me boxes and bags to pack up my things and reminded me, "Be quick, okay?" As I started tearing my room apart, I heard Mom's friends starting to arrive at the front door.

When they saw me, they looked at me with sympathetic eyes that said, '*Oh, you poor child.*' We exchanged quick hellos and some of them hugged me noticeably tight. I didn't want anyone's pity and hated knowing people felt sorry for me. I shrugged it off and knew they were here for the right reasons.

After a short greeting, they all started loading up different parts of the house: the kitchen, the bathroom, the closets, the storage. Mom was running the whole operation. Some things, we realized, hadn't been planned. She contemplated taking the large furniture. It would leave the place empty and we had only planned to take what we needed. However, her friends and her sister convinced her, "*To hell with him!*", and *everything* ended up going into the moving truck. The guys hauled the furniture up and shoved it through the doorway. It was only then that I realized Mom was going to leave Ian with next to nothing. He would come home to an empty house, having nothing but the drapes and carpet.

As I looked around at everything that remained to be packed, I sank into a numbed condition. Ian would be home later that afternoon, and we had to be finished way ahead of his expected arrival. The thought of him arriving home early replayed different scenarios in my mind that completely distracted me. I tried to keep focused on which things I wanted to take with me. My heart was pounding in my chest. Our house was busy with people moving, carrying and lifting things out the door. If Ian had seen what I was looking at, I knew he would punish us all.

The organization I tried to start out with quickly failed and fell apart when I looked around at all the half-filled boxes beginning to stack up in my room. There was no time to pack nicely. My tia, realizing my attempt at organization, helped me pick up the pace by throwing my things into large black bags. Everything just needed to get out the door. Just when I thought I was nearly done, my tia asked me about the things that remained in my room.

"I don't need them, I just packed what I need."

"Well shit, pack the things you don't want too! Just so you don't leave it with him!" She was serious, and that's how everyone in our family felt about Ian. I reopened some bags I thought I was done with and kept filling them up with things I didn't even want or need. It wasn't about what I wanted, or needed, it was about sending Ian a message, a message he had never been given before and it was one I was terrified to deliver.

I watched the clock like a hawk and in record time my room was transformed into an empty space. Even my posters had been taken off the walls. The bags were so packed with clothes, picture frames, books and decorations that I thought they might burst. My closet, once filled to the brim, was nearly empty with only old shoes and clothes that I hadn't worn in years. It started to look like the day we had moved in, and I was reminded of the hope this home once gave us. I laughed to myself at how distant that all seemed now.

The guys trudged in, dripping in sweat, and started disassembling my bed. They carried out my dresser, night stand and lamps; that was the last of it. When I had woken up that morning, my room was in full functioning order. Now, no part of me remained in it at all. Absolutely nothing.

The house was clearing out in lightning speed. Panic continued resonating within me as I walked down the hallway, looking into every bare and empty room. This is what Ian would see when he arrived home: the indents of the furniture on the carpet and nothing in its place.

Once the truck was packed and the work was finished, Caleb and Junior found a way to make light of the situation. When I went downstairs, I found the entire basement trashed with clothes, pictures, old cassettes and other junk piled on the floor that Caleb and Junior had thrown there. Junior laughed and smiled as he tossed the things around. It was his way of saying, "Fuck you, Ian!"

He then went upstairs to celebrate in Caleb's room, and they both tossed a large basket of broken crayons, pens and markers up into the air. I watched them laugh as the crayons shattered around them. They found a stack of papers and did the same. I wanted to be a part of the fun. So I added to the mess by chucking old toys at the walls and watched them shatter into pieces.

The room looked as if a riot had destroyed it. I smiled. After all, this was a celebration. We were leaving. Although there was some joy to be found, I still couldn't give into my emotions until it was all over. I had imagined this day for so long. It was like a happy dream, but now I could barely smile. My face was heavy with worry. I just wanted to leave while we still could with an open doorway and a clear takeoff.

As everyone began to settle and realize there was nothing left to do, they started up their cars and headed to the apartment. Knowing we would not be coming back, Mom checked the house one last time. This would be it. She locked the door, fired up the U-Haul and drove off with everything we owned piled high in the truck. A feeling of relief started sliding into place the further and further we drove away.

I finally could breathe again. The worst was over. There was nothing else we needed to do. All the damage had been done. We were past the point of no return and had moved into a new realm of reality.

We arrived at the new apartment in the afternoon, and some of Mom's friends had to leave. They said their goodbyes and wished us the best of luck. Being a little shorthanded and already exhausted, Mom, Caleb, Junior and I and the remaining friends started to unload.

Moving is never enjoyable. We made what seemed like a thousand trips back and forth from the truck hauling boxes upon boxes up three, long miserable flights of stairs. The truck emptied slowly, but three hours later we were finally finished.

We knew that Ian would be arriving home any minute now. With the little energy I had left, I distracted myself by putting my room in order. As I emptied my things, the moment I had been dreading came. My phone rang.

"Mom, he's calling me. Should I answer it?" I didn't even want to touch my phone.

"No," she said. "No, don't answer it." Mom had already prepared herself. We knew we would have to talk to him, but we all dreaded doing so. We waited and tried to build up our courage.

In just a few short minutes, there were three phone calls and three voice mails. Then Mom's phone started ringing, followed by Caleb's. We knew he wouldn't stop. Eventually we would have to answer him.

He called and called, again and again until finally, Mom answered. She walked into her bedroom and closed the door. Caleb and I were silent, sitting on the carpet of my new room, listening intently through the hollow door.

I heard Mom's cries and a moment later, she opened the door. She came to me, her face drenched in tears and smeared makeup.

"He wants to talk to you." Her hand was shaking as she handed me the phone.

"Me?" I hesitantly took the phone and watched Mom walk away, wiping her tears and saying nothing. Caleb followed behind her, leaving me alone.

"Hello?" I said as my voice trembled.

"Monica?" he said. His voice sounded awful. "What happened?" His words flooded me with incredible sadness.

"We left, Papi." Hearing those words out loud crushed me. I was speechless

"Monica, please talk to me, sweetie. Talk to me baby." He begged, "Please."

"I don't want to talk to you, Papi." I meant it. His voice unleashed such an agony in me that every word he said seemed to smash a bone. Trying to escape, I let the silence stay and listened to his cries. *I did this.*

"Sweetie, please talk to your mother," he pleaded.

"No. I'm not going to convince her of anything. We..." I ruptured into tears, "...We left. We weren't happy." My heart slowly climbed into my throat.

No matter how much I had wanted this, no matter how much I had supported it, helped it, planned it and encouraged it, I felt like none of it mattered. I felt awful. *I'm an awful person, no better than him.* I just wanted to leave. I didn't want to hurt anyone. We only wanted to be happy. And now, I questioned whether it was all worth it and why we had to leave this way.

I expected him to be livid. I expected him to yell, to scream, to threaten us, to confirm why we had left in the first place. But he did none of that. If he had, it would have been easier to believe in our choice, but instead, he only cried, the deepest cry I ever heard from him. An emotion I didn't even know he had poured from his heart. Guilt was drowning me, and I felt all the more terrible for thinking the decision we had made was a good one.

When I could say nothing more, he asked to speak to Caleb.

"Caleb!" I yelled and handed him the phone. He took it and walked out of my room. I closed the door behind him and slowly walked to my dresser. I laid my hands on top of it and looked up at myself in the mirror. I watched my tears fall and noticed the crinkles of my face as I wept. I slowed my breathing and wiped my face. *What have we just done?* I was ashamed for hurting someone so badly. My logic told me that it was the right choice. But that didn't stop me from hurting and feeling like an ugly person. I hadn't expected to feel all this pain and agony.

Maybe, it wasn't leaving that hurt. It was accepting that even after all the pain he inflicted, all the terror he had brought and all the fear he put into my heart, I still loved him. I didn't understand how I could still love someone like that, or how I could have any hope for him after everything he had done to us. Maybe I was mistaking love for pity. Maybe I was too young to tell the difference.

At the same time, I knew there were no simple options. There was never going to be an easy way out of this. There was nothing that would ever satisfy him enough so that we could all walk away in peace. I could think of no other way out. I realized I loved him, but I loved Mom more and where she went, my heart followed.

She sat and talked with Ian on the phone for hours.

"No, Ian. No!" she said firmly. "I can't be with you. I love you, but…" I focused, trying to hear him on the other side of the call.

"No, you're never going to change," she continued, "You're always going to be the way you are. I've had enough." She paused.

"No, I don't want to try anything. We are done." She spoke without hesitation, "We are done! The kids aren't happy. I'm not happy!" Her voice rose, "No! They're scared of you. They are scared."

They went on this way until the sun set. She had spent the

entire evening on the phone with him, trying to explain why she had made the choice she did and why there was no other way but to leave. But her words seemed to be falling on deaf ears. He only urged her to reconsider and to make one final try. But it was just like all the other final tries they'd had. She agreed to nothing. She was forcing him to see that she stood strong in her decision, but he couldn't accept her strength.

When she finally ended the call, she opened the door and sat back down on the bed, aware we were anxiously waiting. Caleb and I went in to comfort her with hugs and kisses, brushing her bangs out of the way and peeling the strands of hair away from her wet face. I saw the strength she was trying to keep. As a family, we sat together in the dark room and held one another closely, feeling safe in each other's arms.

"We're doing the right thing, Mom. It's okay," I said. I noticed her tears were beginning to fade, and she hugged us both tight as we sat on the bed with her for a while longer; the day's stress was finally coming to an end.

It was late, and we were all drained. A silence filled the air as we started to get ready for bed, each of us replaying the moments of the day. As I watched every moment over and over again in my mind, I couldn't believe we had actually done it.

For the first night since Ian had returned from prison, I took a peaceful shower and rested easy, knowing we were all safe.

...

The living room was set up with a television, the kitchen with dishes and the table with a centerpiece. We began to settle into this new life. It quickly became our little home. The move brought changes I had never considered. Now that she had reclaimed the role of sole provider, Mom was back to being overrun with work. With the main street nearby, Caleb and I were to keep out of its sight. That meant no bike riding or walking in sight of anyone who would be driving on the road. Mom didn't have to explain how much there was to lose and the danger we would face if he ever discovered where we lived.

Mom filed for divorce and was waiting for Ian to sign the paperwork, a task we knew immediately would cause problems. My feelings were confirmed when I listened to her argue day after day with him over the phone about how he was going to change. He kept telling her he was going to be a different man, that we could be a family again, and blah blah blah. It was like listening to a child tell a lie, and I didn't want to hear it anymore.

The initial stress of the move slowly dispersed, and the summer invited relaxation and peace of mind. We began to enjoy the freedom we had worked so hard to achieve. With only three months of good summer weather, we made the most of it.

We traveled to the Michigan Dunes for a beach day to bask in the sun with Mom's friend Evan and his children. We traveled to Wisconsin to lodge at the indoor water park resorts. We went out for movies, for dinners, and did just about anything that allowed us to enjoy the warm night air. Mom loved the summer; it was the time when she shined best. Even in the blistering high 90s, she refused to put the a/c on.

I began to notice we were having all of this fun with the same friend, Evan. Mom seemed to be spending most of her spare time with him. He was a soft spoken, six-foot, clean cut man who had a tender look in his eyes when he gazed at her.

By the time I knew anything about their relationship, they were already over a year into dating and much closer than I realized.

I noticed her smile shining an awful lot and she paid more attention than usual to her makeup and choice of clothes. She was giggly, upbeat and spontaneous. She laughed more than I had ever seen with her smile stretching from ear to ear. It was no secret anymore, and it didn't need to be. Mom had a boyfriend.

I was told she met him at her job where he worked as a security guard. Her friends told me how they would sneak away for lunch together, making it obvious they were flirting across the table by the smiles they couldn't keep from their faces. I knew they were telling me the truth, because I could see Mom's eyes light up when he was around. She no longer looked like a mom, but a woman head over heels for a man. It was a sight that filled my heart's cup.

After every outing with Evan and his two daughters, Mom was eager to get our feedback. "Soooo, what do you guys think of Evan?"

"He seems really nice. He seems to like you a lot." Although I hadn't formed much of an opinion yet, I knew she was happier than I had ever seen her. That was all he needed to do to have my approval. I could tell Mom was excited by even the simplest praise of him. He was the topic of all her conversations.

"Do you think it's weird that he doesn't like to hold hands?" she asked. I was surprised she wanted advice from a sixteen-year-old. We gossiped during the car ride home while Caleb listened to music in the back seat, unable to be a part of girl talk. Mom knew I was in my first serious relationship, too, so we dished the dirt back and forth on our boys. It was a milestone in our mother-daughter relationship.

She told me that Evan's fiftieth birthday was coming up, and she had big plans that would need our help. She took me over to the venue for my opinion. Mickadoon's was a private party rental space lined with booth seating, a dance floor and a bowling alley with a bar just next door. I could see the excitement spilling out of her as she pointed to where the decorations would go, where the cake would be set up, where the DJ would be, and where everyone would be waiting to scream *SURPRISE* when he walked in. She booked it before we left and started secretly inviting all their friends.

I had never seen Mom plan something with that amount of enthusiasm, aside from our childhood birthday parties. She was glowing with excitement as the party drew near. Her schedule was filled with projects and plans I'd never seen her take on before. She had booked herself a vacation to Arizona and Las Vegas to visit her godparents. I had not seen them since the night they welcomed us into their home after the shooting on Mozart. She was gone for two and a half weeks and when she returned, she had glorious stories about the Grand Canyon and the wild Vegas strip. She brought me back a gold chain necklace with a white heart on the end that had my name on it and a keychain with a black and gold letter M from the MGM Grand hotel. Just a few short weeks after her vacation, it was time for Evan's party.

All of our friends arrived early to set up and take positions. The place was filled with fiftieth birthday decorations, and more than twenty of us gathered together while Mom went out to greet him in the parking lot. As he walked through the door, he was bombarded with everyone shouting *Surprise!* The thrill on

Mom's face said she knew all of her efforts had paid off.

The party was a success, and everyone had done their part to make it so. The lights flashed, the music grew louder, and everyone went in for second helpings on cake. With Caleb, Nikki and my other friends invited too, I was enjoying it, but not as much as Mom. Her face was radiating happiness every time I looked at her. The party was flowing.

After our last distressing conversation, I barely had any communication with Ian, and I never saw him. I had stopped answering his calls, and he finally stopped making them. His communication was mainly with Mom. I wondered what he was doing with his life. It couldn't have been nearly as impressive as what Mom was doing with hers.

As I saw Mom's heart move towards Evan, I still felt remorse for leaving Ian the way we did. I hoped that he was doing better, that he, too, could find peace and live a happier life. Although I wished the best for him, I had learned never to expect anything either.

Mom told us Ian was going to church every Sunday asking for forgiveness and seeing a therapist regularly. Whether he was being honest or not, she had assured him this didn't mean they were getting back together again. She told him he should only go if it was for his benefit and his benefit alone. Well, he continued to go, and he even asked us to join him.

Perhaps Mom's happiness with Evan clouded her better judgment, because she agreed to attend a service with him. As Mom dragged us along to church that weekend, I was more than a little upset. In what should be a place of peace, I sat on high wild alert, muting the pastor's words and hawking at Ian's every move, every expression and every smile. I was never certain if he was being genuine or putting on another good-boy act. *Was this another mask?* I had seen it evaporate into thin air as soon as something triggered him. In order to avoid ever falling victim again, I simply never believed him. I couldn't.

After church, I asked Mom never to take us again and thankfully, she never did.

No matter what he said, he was slowly trying to win us back. I knew he couldn't have known how pointless his efforts really were. Mom had moved on with her life and was happily thriving. There was nothing he could do that would have ever convinced me we should go back to him and, truth be told, I wouldn't have believed him anyway.

His reign in our lives was becoming no more than a pile of distant memories which were slowly being replaced with better ones. Fear was being replaced with peace; pain with freedom; and tears with smiles.

Never was I ever letting it go again.

...

Questions. No answers.

August 2008

ARRIVING BACK TO START A NEW SCHOOL YEAR was anything but exciting. As everyone in class exchanged stories about their summer and all its glamour, I tried to stay on other topics. With the peace of the summer gone, work and school became top priority. Mom was picking up shifts nearly every night of every day. When she actually had a night off, she spent it in front of the TV with a good movie she managed to get ten minutes into before falling asleep. Her constant absence was something I had been used to and now my seventeen-year-old mind saw it as an opportunity.

I don't know how I became friends with some of the riskier kids of my class, but they helped me connect the dots. With Mom gone most the time, they realized they had a free place to stay almost every weekend. It started out innocently, just three or four friends a night and a stolen case of beer. Word spread like a forest fire and suddenly, I started gaining lots of friends. Mom would leave about 10:30 PM and all my new friends would trickle in about 11:00.

Each time there was a party, and more and more people began to show. I drank more and cared less until one night I blacked out entirely. I couldn't function well enough to gather my words and tell everyone to keep the noise down or to clean up their spilled beer from the carpet as they played beer pong in the kitchen. The only thing I remember seeing was a swarm of people that I hadn't invited arrive later in the night. After that, everything fades back into an obliterated state.

When a friend woke me up the next morning, I was surprised to find I was wearing my coat. I reached into my pockets to find crumpled McChicken wrappers and had no recollection of how they got there. The sun was rising, and I was nowhere close to being sober.

"Isn't your mom coming home soon?" my friend asked, but I was still too drunk to respond. Mom was going to be home from work at 8:00 AM, and I looked around to see all the girls cleaning the apartment from top to bottom. They were wiping down tables, chairs and counters and picking up beer tabs and trash. I noticed they already had two large bags filled. The place seemed to be in perfect order when they left, so I dragged myself off the couch and into my bed to make it seem as if I had been there all night. I laid there and within minutes of closing my eyes, I heard keys clinking at the door. I got into character. I heard Mom rustling through the entrance with all her belongings.

"What is that smell?" I heard her whisper. *Dammit! Oh well, it's over.* She then cracked open my door.

"Monica," she whispered. "Monica!"

I made a little noise as I laid there, "Hmmm?"

"Are you okay?" she whispered.

"Yeah, why?" It was not the question I expected her to ask, but I played along.

"Are you sleeping?"

"Yeah," I said, trying to appear disrupted.

"Okay." Then she closed the door. *Pheww!* I thought, *I got away with it.* Or so I believed for the next five years.

My father eventually provided me with a reality check that I never really got away with anything. Mom apparently had called him later that day in a full rage. She was livid after putting the pieces together herself.

"You'll never believe what this girl did!" she told him.

"What?"

"She had a party when I was at work! I could ring her neck!"

Being the casual parent, his response was, "She's a kid, kids are gonna do stupid things."

Stupid, indeed. After I had sensed that Mom knew something was up, I put a stop to the parties before it all blew up in my face. They were getting out of control for me, and I really couldn't do the lying part. Even though it was hard to speak up for myself and tell all my new friends no, I cherished my relationship with Mom and still had a great deal of respect for her. So, even if it meant losing all the friends I had just made, it was worth it. It meant there would be at least one less person in the world that she hadn't lost respect for.

...

November 2008

133

That period of time was the riskiest part of my teenage life. There was much that happened that I'm not particularly proud of, but it all came to an end when I met Jim. Just when I thought I had familiarized myself with everyone in the school, I met a guy in my history class whom I had never seen before. Like many young loves that take flight, we began texting every minute of every day. After a few short weeks, I was in my first real relationship. Jim and I became quickly infatuated with one another and our emotions spiraled high. I immediately became a happier person. However, as I began to flaunt my happiness around, I noticed that Mom was no longer flaunting hers.

Something was wrong. Her shining had become clouded. She waited a while before eventually telling me that she and Evan had broken up. By then, her glow seemed to have completely disappeared. She didn't want to say much, and although I was curious for details, I didn't push her. She only told me how he was less than appreciative for the party and he decided to move away. As a result, being at work with him was really awkward.

Their break up was blindsiding. From the outside, they appeared to be reaching for the stars. I was still getting to know Evan, and I didn't know him well enough to understand what may have caused their break up. As much as I wanted to take all her pain and self-destructive questioning away, there was nothing I could do for her. It made me feel helpless and reminded me that I couldn't control things in other people's lives. It wasn't my life. It was hers.

Knowing little to nothing about their split left me asking questions I had no answers to: *What's his problem?! They seemed so good together, what happened?! Why is this happening to her?*

Up until that time, Mom and I had been incredibly close. We looked out for each other and had been continually honest with one another. We conversed about life, love and family and had gone to one another for advice on almost every topic possible. But it seemed as if life slowly started building barriers between us after Evan left.

As I was engulfed with my new love, she was recovering from hers. She didn't open up anymore. She no longer kept us in the loop with her plans, her feelings, and her personal life. She stopped doing all the things that made her thrive: going out, getting her nails and hair done, taking trips. So much stopped, and I realized I had no idea what was going on in her life anymore. And she had no idea of what was happening in mine. A change began to seep in, and I could sense the distance forming between all of us.

Spending all my hours with Jim meant I was oblivious to everything happening at home. Coming home from school one day, I was walking up the flight of stairs and turned the corner to the third floor. I could hear shouting and yelling coming from the end of the hall. As I got closer, I realized it was coming from our apartment. I opened the door to see Caleb shouting at Mom. He was yelling at the top of his lungs in a way I had never seen before. We had all tested Mom's patience at one point or another, but this was different.

I must have come at the end of their argument because Caleb was so enraged that he ran out the door and down the hall. With no idea why he had left, I went down the hall after him, but he was gone.

I came back to the apartment to find Mom, sitting in the dark on her bed in quiet tears. It was the second time I heard her question her ability to be a good Mom. The first time happened before our move, after a similar challenging argument with one of my brothers. I had walked upstairs in that house after she had the argument. She was sitting at the end of the bed with her head down, crying softly. I quietly walked in and sat next to her, hugging her and brushing away her curls.

"Am I a bad mother?" she asked. Her question both shocked me and saddened me as I looked at her red face. I couldn't believe she would even ask such a question.

"No! Of course not," I answered. We talked for a few moments as I reassured her she was crazy for asking such ridiculous things.

She replied smiling, "I'm so glad I have a girl. Why couldn't you be the oldest?" Her words made me feel both special and sad. Even then, however, she doubted all her noble efforts and questioned her ability as a mother. Now, she looked up at me with the same tear drenched face I couldn't bear to see. And although he was out of line, it felt hypocritical for me to defend Caleb's actions when I had been so secretly defiant. Instead, I held her hand, rubbed her back, and placed my head on her shoulder, allowing the moment to calm. By the end of our conversation, she finally had a true smile. She dried all her tears and held me tightly.

It was during these months that life started becoming unkind to Mom; and none of our actions were of any help either. There was her recently ended relationship; my secretive night life, Caleb's defiance, and Junior's inability to keep a job. On top of all that was her growing financial stress. It was these obstacles, I believe, that caused Mom to begin losing sight of her path. I think she was beginning to feel as if all of her control was slipping away.

I know she felt backed into a corner. The same day after Caleb ran out of the apartment, all of her emotions surfaced in my presence. After Mom dried her tears and gathered her strength, she and I got in her car to search for Caleb. I sat in the passenger seat, still and silent, as she cursed the heavens and begged the Lord for patience, guidance and the answers she desperately wanted. She drove enraged, and it was the angriest I had ever seen her. She shouted and swore more in those few minutes then she had in all the years I'd been alive. After we went aimlessly around the block with no sign of Caleb, she gave up and drove back to the apartment.

She parked the car and took out the keys. Just when I thought she was calm, she unleashed a loud, bloodcurdling cry that rang in my ears and echoed in the small confined space of her car. Furious, she began thrashing the steering wheel over and over again and slamming her hands on the dashboard in a frantic rage. She seemed to have so much strength that I thought she could have torn the steering wheel clean off the car.

"What do I do? Huh?" she screamed, "What do I do with you guys?" She stared at me, her eyes pouring with tears and an anger I didn't recognize. It seemed I was to provide the solution she needed as she searched desperately for answers. Her anger terrified me, and I drew myself into the corner of my seat, thinking she might hit me. When she had nothing left, she sat with her hands over her face crying. I had no words for her, and I knew I couldn't comfort her.

I had been witness to Ian's rage millions of times, but never Mom's. It frightened me. I didn't understand what she was going through. I couldn't even begin to make sense of it, and for that brief moment in her car, I didn't even know who she was. All I could understand was that she was angrier than ever before, and she was demanding answers I didn't have. I only wanted to take back everything I had ever done that was wrong and prevent anyone from doing anything else to her.

...

After that day, I treaded lightly in my actions. I never wanted to see her like that again. Although I didn't understand her pain, I knew I didn't want to make it worse.

In just a few short months everything seemed to have crumpled in our lives. Our light-hearted conversations became hostile arguments. Our laughable car rides became a time for warnings of discipline as she vocalized her disdain for our deplorable behavior. No one was listening to anyone or abiding by Mom's rules. No one was taking her seriously. Instead, we defied all her boundaries. Though, as life would have it, none of our actions had a single thing to do with what happened next.

I was coming home from school and walked into the apartment. I put my things down and when I looked up I was struck with fear. Ian was sitting in the living room, casually watching television dressed in jeans and a sweater; calm as could be. He even greeted me with a "Hey!" which I didn't respond to.

My body was paralyzed for a moment before I could make up my mind about what to do. *Was I alone?* I inched my head around the corner to see Mom in the bathroom, who appeared entirely composed. It felt like I was waking up in the middle of a terrible nightmare. I didn't know the beginning of it and I didn't want to know the end. She must have known I was home, because she shut off the light and came to the living room. Ian stood up, turned off the TV, and she walked him to the doorway. I stood puzzled while they barely acknowledged my presence.

"Mom, where are you going?" I said, as if I was the parent.

"I'll be right back," she said as she left, barely looking at me.

When she closed the door, I began pacing like a caged animal. I pinched myself just to make sure I was awake, to make sure I actually saw Ian watching TV in our apartment. *You know, the apartment we snuck away to. The apartment we searched and searched for just to get out!* My mind couldn't handle the questions and my body was in a state of panic. As I waited for Mom to return, I must have asked myself a thousand questions that I wanted her to answer.

Thankfully, she returned a few minutes later and relieved my wild thoughts. As she took off her things in the entry way, I stood like an angry parent in the kitchen with both hands firmly on the counter.

"Mom, why was he here?" I had never been so serious. I wanted a straight answer, but her avoidance only made me angrier. I grew louder.

"Mom!" I was shaking with anger, desperate for her to speak. "Why was he HERE?"

She paused for a moment before she spoke, "Papi and I are getting back together."

Her words brought to the surface unimaginable wrath that fueled every part of my being. "WHAT?" I shouted. I couldn't control myself and to be truthful, I can't even remember the conversation that followed because as she spoke, my enraged thoughts blocked her out. I was furious, absolutely livid, and in complete denial. *No, she didn't just say what I thought she said. Please! She didn't just say what I thought she said!*

If you've been through traumatic experiences that have changed your life in worse ways than most people are able to comprehend, then you know that the mind and body are able to initiate a preservation mode. It is a mode that protects you and doesn't allow you to remember those terrible moments. For me, this was one of those moments. I believe we lose those awful memories because our body is using huge amounts of energy on the emotions that are consuming it, so the body intentionally tells other, less important functions, to shut off, including memory. The body is a remarkable instrument. It's smart enough to know, *hey, you're not gonna wanna remember this anyway. Let's just turn that off, too*. It realizes that what's most crucial in those life changing seconds is releasing the toxic levels of emotional chaos that are drowning you to death. Although I have some psychology education, I'm no doctor nor any type of licensed official. I'm simply a person with a theory based on the many terrible experiences I have lived through.

...

In the days and weeks that followed, there was an inexplicable driving force that came from the pit of my soul that compelled me to convince her to change the horrendous choice she had made. At the top of my lungs, I yelled, screamed and argued with her in every waking second. I followed her everywhere, never giving it a rest. I knowingly and willingly overstepped all my boundaries, using any approach possible in hopes of changing her mind. I followed her in the kitchen, in the bath-room, in the bedroom, in the car, in the laundry room, and even at the grocery store when people were around us. Anywhere I had a second of her attention, I tried to convince her not to return to Ian.

My will was strong. I had no intention of letting it go. I made it my mission to do everything in my power to stop this nightmare from happening all over again.

"You can't, Mom, you just can't! After everything we did to get away! You can't go back! I don't want to go back! I'm not going. I can't believe you would even want to go back! Why? WHY! Why do you want to go back?" I asked, shouting over any word she tried to get in to justify her actions.

Every time I demanded answers, she comprised a new one. Her reasoning was scattered and I don't even believe that she believed it herself. She explained how the finances were getting out of control, and the opportunity arose for her to become Ian's disabled mother's power of attorney. That meant she could handle her monthly income. She told me how managing all of us kids had grown too difficult and too stressful. And although she never said it, I know she was angry at me for having been so secretive with my parties. She said she was lonely since Evan left and needed someone to take care of her. She confessed how Ian was relentlessly begging her to come back, and how his time with the church and priest made him a changed man.

I wasn't convinced for a moment. There was no reason in the world to do what she was about to do. I couldn't accept anything she said, and I wasn't going to stop fighting this until I was blue in the face. I couldn't accept any other answer than, *Okay, I won't go back*. I desperately wanted to hear the words, but she never said them.

It wasn't until years later that I discovered Ian had indeed received the divorce paperwork. Unfortunately, he had received them with our new apartment address and came to find Mom in the parking lot. So, as fate would have it, his action had nothing to do with any of us.

My own persistence drove me insane. Sparking all this confrontation became too stressful for both of us. To find some peace, I racked up more Jim time and left whenever she let me. I didn't want to go back to the old home. But I couldn't stand to be in the apartment either, because every time I saw Mom, I fought her tooth and bleeding nail about her choice.

Everything happened quicker than I could digest. Within weeks of Mom's decision to go back, Ian surpassed crawling and simply thrusted himself back into our lives. He had taken comfort in our apartment and came over to sleep, to eat, to watch television, or just to be there. I said nothing and pretended he didn't exist.

In no time at all, he built back the walls of tension, fear and control. He was already arguing with Junior, Caleb and me. He invaded our space, with Mom's permission, and was controlling Mom's heart. As a result, any hope of changing Mom's decision slipped further and further away.

During a night she was at work, the way-too-nice side of me let Ian know I was going out with Jim. I told him I would be back later and headed for the door. He sat on the couch with only the light of the television flashing upon his stern face, and he calmly replied, "No." I paused and knew exactly what he was doing. It was the same thing all over again. Anywhere he could force his hand, he did. Later on, he grounded me for one week for getting home at 2:01 AM. The curfew was 2:00 AM. This merry-go-round was getting old for me, and I was tired of his games.

I called Mom at work to tell her what he was trying to pull and was astounded to hear that she agreed with him. By her orders, I had to listen to him. My heart was broken; not because we had to obey him, but because I could tell we were losing her again. Ian had been back less than a month, and already he had effortlessly caught her in his paralyzing trance which she willingly walked into.

I closed my door and stared at the floor, baffled as I hung up the phone with Mom. *Why is this happening?* I texted Jim, who was waiting patiently downstairs.

My blood must have boiled to five hundred degrees as I lay in bed shaking in anger. I texted Jim to tell him how sorry I was to have left him waiting for so long. I couldn't believe this was happening, nor did I understand how it happened or when it happened! Ian was sitting in the next room watching TV on a couch we had swiped from under him just seven months ago. He was already telling me what I could and couldn't do. He continually belittled me and was referring to all of us as *dysfunctional* for not obeying him. Overflowing with emotions and thoughts that I couldn't make sense of, I went from quiet crying to punching my walls. Sometimes I would find myself screaming, and other times I would be begging the Lord for help. Even though I told myself it would be okay, I knew that I was lying. I felt as helpless as a wounded baby calf running from the inevitable attack of the lions. Ian had returned to our lives, and Mom allowed it.

...

December 2008

The weeks I spent arguing with Mom proved useless. In no time at all, she had planned to move back into the house after Christmas. Neither Caleb nor I were in a cheerful, holiday spirit. Mom spent Christmas Eve working all night while Caleb and I opened our one gift at midnight. After enduring the last few months, I knew we didn't even deserve the single gift that sat on the evergreen skirt below our cheerless tree.

I opened up a small red box to find the black, iPod Classic 80gb I had asked for. I fired it up and raced for the computer to lather it up in my favorite music. We called Mom at work and thanked her graciously with excitement, but in short simple words she said, *you're welcome, love you* and then went back to work. Her tone made me feel like an awful daughter.

After the holidays, Mom, Caleb and I went to visit our tia and cousins. We were all gathered in my tia's living room when I saw another opportunity to chime in on the up and coming move. Although it was scheduled just weeks away, I hadn't let the hope of changing her mind die just yet. Mom was discussing the move with her sister when I boldly interrupted.

"Titi tell her! Tell her she can't go back. This is ridiculous!" I exclaimed. "I feel like this is going to be our last chance, ya know? Like we're trying this for the third time!" I couldn't put into words what I felt. I only knew that I had a deep, unsettling feeling about it. To me, I saw it as our third try with Ian. We had left once, which was hard enough, and something told me we wouldn't get another chance to leave again. Inside, my heart was shouting *NO! Don't do it!*

But to my great disappointment, Tia Carlita looked at me with deep sympathy and replied, "Sweetie, it's her decision. It's her life and her choice." She continued with her reasoning, but I stopped on her words and became lost in my baffled thoughts sprinting into chaos. I began to question my own sanity and felt as if all my efforts had been defeated.

...

Around Mom, Ian was in full character and only showed her the side of him that he wanted her to see. Smiling and affectionate, he played the familiar role that had won our hearts the first time. He had convinced her that they would make this a real fresh start and to prove it, they were going to remodel the house together. He persuaded her to come over so they could brainstorm ideas for the kitchen which she asked to be done first. Caleb and I rode with them in the back seat to the hideous barn house, now fouler to me than ever.

As we walked inside, I was taken right back to the day we left. The house was just as pitiful and empty as when we left it. Crayons even still covered the floor of Caleb's old room. There was still no furniture and nowhere to sit. It was as if Ian knew he had no reason to move on.

I sat outside the kitchen on the living room carpet as they conversed and dreamt up their ideas. They discussed colors, textures, design and costs. They started making plans: when to start, where to go for supplies, when they thought it would be finished, everything. It looked as if they were playing house like two children. It made me sick. I listened but had no expectation that they would do any of those things.

Instead, I only sensed his lure pulling her in closer, but Mom didn't seem to notice a thing. She was so far beyond my help and was behaving as if she was in a hypnotized state or under a terrible curse, just taking in all the sweet words that slithered from his mouth. Smiling and laughing together, they kept on, even beginning to flirt and giggle. I lost it.

"This is stupid!" I blurted. My relentless anger erupted into screams, and the tears began to pour.

They darted out of the kitchen and stared at me sitting on the floor. Ian appeared upset that I had derailed their fun and Mom shook her head with distress and confusion. Using every ounce of determination within me, I was going to take off his mask one way or another.

Whether Mom saw it or not, all I cared about was getting her out of her own mistake. I didn't care what they thought of me or how childish I appeared. I was going to try one last time to prevent this all from coming true.

"This is SO, SO STUPID!" I shouted. "We're moving back to this stupid house? With him? I hate it! I hate it here! You can't get back together, you can't!" After each tear I wiped, there came another.

For a moment, they seemed speechless until Ian shouted, "She can go live with her father if she's gonna act like this!" He then lit up a cigarette and stormed out the front door. Mom stood in front of me, silent, almost as if she had no idea what to do with what I said.

I don't know what I expected would happen, but my outburst didn't get anywhere near the reaction I had hoped for. I felt my efforts were falling on stone souls and after that, I was out of ideas. In that moment, I had poured my true feelings out for them to hear and tried to become the biggest obstacle in their reunion. *Now what!* But it was like trying to make waves in an empty pool. It wasn't my life. My Tia was right; it was Mom's life. It was Mom's choice. I had all the questions in the world, but not a single answer to any of them.

...

The Third Return

January 2009

MOVING DAY. There's that moment again. The one where your emotions are so intense your body needs to shut down other important functions just to make sure you don't internally combust. Yes. That moment. And it came again before the end of the month.

I was packing up my room in the apartment and watching as the space began to empty all over again. I was defeated and overpowered by what I knew were lies and deception. I had no desire to leave the place that had been our saving grace and give up the freedom we had found from the panic, draining anxiety and mind-boggling stress that always came with Ian. Now, living with him, it would all return.

Somehow, he had managed to return again and for the life of me, I couldn't comprehend why Mom had allowed it. She was set on her choice and with plans in motion, I saw no point in fighting it anymore.

After years of watching her disregard her own peace in

order to keep others happy, I came to adapt the same behavior. Even though I'm like her in nearly all my ways, Ian's return made me sick and nauseous. I could see his mask fading before she could.

...

The ability to speak up for myself has always been my greatest challenge. To speak up for one's self is a talent I thought I would never have. Instead, I was taught to be obedient, to listen, and to do as you're told. I was always instructed to obey respectfully and without question by my Catholic school, by Mom, by Ian, and by my family. Everyone stuffed me to the brim with firm directions on how to listen, shut it and zip it. These lessons had been so deeply engraved in me, that I never considered I had other options. As a result, I grew up to become a person who had not the slightest clue of how to make decisions for myself.

Essentially, I became a pushover and let people wipe their spiked combat boots all over me. It was a quality in me that I labeled as being very flawed, but it was nothing I could even begin to change. Not alone, at least.

Even when returning to Ian, I believed everyone was right and I was the crazy, out-of-line one for refusing to go back to this man for the third time. Yet, even though my heart was telling me this was the worst decision we could ever make, my mind told me *hey, you're not listening* and *hey, you need to do what the adults are telling you to do. Stop it already. Listen! Obey!*

So I did. I started packing up. I tore down my posters again. I packed up my clothes again. I even asked Jim to help. I submitted to Ian's power and said nothing during the move.

...

One crucial lesson life has revealed to me time and time again is that adults can be wrong just like children can be. Grown adults are simply children in adult bodies, still learning about the world themselves. Yes, they know a thing or two. Yes, you can learn from them. If they're one hundred and two years old, indeed yes, listen to their wisdom.

However, it can be foolish to think that children don't possess the capacity to teach someone at any age something about the world. Something about yourself.

Yet, being the wise adults we believe ourselves to be, we allow our own ignorance to divide us. We ignore what children have to say if it goes against the lessons we've had in our own, more experienced lives. We immediately jump to the argument that, "I'm older and I know better," or "This happened to me, so it will surely happen to you." Which may be true in many circumstances, but don't let that dominate your view into believing you have life figured out for you *and* your children.

The word "youth" is often misrepresented as being immature or being an amateur. It goes against our idea of wisdom to view young ones as teachers and guides in the same way we view our elders. Life's lessons come in various ways. This kind of closed-mindedness blocks the access of new information, new lessons that life may be trying to teach you through your child: lessons that may really and truly benefit you. Why else would life be trying to give them to you?

Acknowledge when you're wrong and tell them if you are! This not only removes the divide and invites unity but teaches children valuable lessons about transparency. Trying to be all high and mighty just to show them you are perfect helps no one grow. Is perfection the reality of the world? You know it's not. We're all flawed, working on our flaws every day. They won't benefit from lies or half-truths. Show them the real, even ugly side of life. I'd be willing to bargain that they already know far more about what happens in the dark than you think.

...

All those new, exciting feelings one might have when moving into a new place were entirely nonexistent. The house was not a home, but a reminder of what we once had to do in order to leave it and who we were trying to leave. It was a lingering memory of where we once were, and where I feared we'd be again.

Ian was still putting on his caring, compassionate son act and assuring Mom this was the best thing for his mother and that she had made the right choice. He convinced her that church had helped him change more than ever before, and this was their opportunity to start a new life.

It wasn't long before the kitchen started to be remodeled with a new black backsplash and grey countertops. Caleb moved into my old room, while Grandma moved into his old one. That left me to take the dreary, dark wooden basement Junior had been kicked out of.

After leaving the apartment, Junior was gone again and was now living with our tias or wherever he could. And here we were again, feeding Ian's control. I suspected it wouldn't take long before his old ways shined in all their horrible glory. The night he came home from prison had engraved a strong lesson in me to never let myself believe for a single, solitary second that he was ever capable of changing.

My Ian-instincts told me to be on alert, but inside I had lost all respect for him. Like a hopeless soul, I was dangling at my edge. At every moment, I was prepared to revolt if he tried to start with me. If I made him angry, so be it. I was angry enough just living under the same roof. I no longer cared about treading his dark waters and instead, decided I would cannonball right in. I feared him, but my fear for Mom was greater.

After settling in, Jim started coming over to the house to spend time together. It quickly became uncomfortable with Ian sitting in the living room watching television outside my room. On one particular night, Ian demanded that I keep my door open when Jim came over. I looked at him, puzzled, because he seemed convinced an open door would stop me from who-knows what. It didn't. A few minutes after Jim arrived, we started making out on my bed. When moving around on the bed became too noisy, we took a risk and moved to the floor. We continued for a second longer, and I lost all sense of caring at all. Every sensation was focused on Jim and the hypnotic love I was in.

I should have known Ian was keeping his radar on because the sudden slam of the laundry door threw me right off of Jim. I looked up and only saw the back of Ian's head trailing off to the living room. I wondered if he saw me, but since it was never like Ian to stay quiet when he was angry, I looked at Jim with a smile of relief.

I figured Jim and I had become a little too quiet. If Ian

was already suspicious, I didn't want to push my luck. Jim and I cooled off and talked, playing games and showing each other new music for the next couple hours.

When it came time for Jim to go home, I stood outside the front door on the single stone step under the moonlight's glow with my arms around his neck. I kissed him goodbye for longer than anyone needs to say goodbye, then returned inside. My heart was like a floating cloud. Just as I closed the door, Mom was coming up the stairs. Since I had caught a second of her time, I asked her if I could go to a concert the next week with Jim.

I didn't know he was nearby, but Ian erupted from the kitchen screaming and pointing his finger at me, "You're not going anywhere! You're grounded!"

Mom and I looked at each other confused. "Grounded? What did she do?" Mom asked as she turned around.

"She was acting like a little slut! She was all over him down there!" He didn't bother to look at Mom and instead kept his stern eyes on me. Mom turned towards me, and I was embarrassed for her to discover what I had done.

Mom's eyes softened, "Honey is that true?" she spoke gently. I was about to speak, but before I got a word out, Ian screamed at me again, "She was on the floor! All over him!"

"Okay, Ian," Mom said sternly, trying to take over the problem. But I felt heat rising inside and something took control of me. I didn't want him talking to me like this anymore and I wasn't going to let him, either. Whatever I screamed at him, something about him not being my real father, made him lose the little composure he had. He leaped off the top of the stairs, stomped on the floor, and came within inches of my face.

He was so enraged that his spit sprayed all over my face as he screamed at me.

I stood staring into his eyes, yelling back. As we stood in the doorway, escalating each other's fury, Mom came between us and pushed Ian further and further away from me. She was struggling with all her strength, and eventually she got him up to the top of the stairs. I stared at him, disgusted. His eyes held mine as he continued to shout profanities at me from the top of the steps.

I could see Mom was trying to pull him to their bedroom, so I released my stare and bolted downstairs. I slammed my bedroom door, threw myself on my bed, and listened to Mom in the bedroom above me trying to calm him down.

I lay staring at the ceiling, listening to Mom's soothing voice. I hadn't given any thought to whether I was in the wrong or not, but Ian's constant insults, belittling and degradation had become enough. I was exhausted from fearing him and his manipulative ability to take advantage of it. To me, Ian was the bully I needed to stand up to. I was only sorry I had involved Mom.

The next few weeks I spent grounded in my room. I did nothing but go to school and come straight home. I told Jim about what happened, and we both agreed it'd be best that he no longer came over. I still didn't understand if I was right in all of this, but after all the incredible damage that Ian had done, I didn't think respecting him mattered anymore. I had none left for him, and I felt my respect for Mom slipping too.

Riveting anger and resentment told me that it was because of her that Ian was here in the first place. I didn't want to be angry at Mom. I loved her, but I couldn't help resenting her choice.

Days later, she told me that she and Evan had started seeing each other again. When she told me that, the little respect I had lost for her flourished back into full-grown love. She told me they had gotten back together within weeks of us moving back in with Ian, and I couldn't understand why she had been pretending this whole time. Sweet relief swam through my veins, and I was grateful to know she wasn't truly committed to Ian in the way she had made it seem. *Thank goodness!* Her trance-like curse seemed to have been lifted. She stopped acting in Ian's play and came back to her happier, assertive, more reasonable self. Her light had been lit and she became Mom again.

Mom knew that her every decision heavily impacted me. When she was in a bad place, I was in a bad place. When she was happy, I was happy. So when Mom started becoming secretly happy, radiant and glowing again, even with Ian lurking in our lives, I too, became happier, knowing her heart was not with him. Seeing her joy somehow made dealing with Ian easier.

People are sometimes very quick to judge, especially when it comes to other peoples' relationships. The topic people like to throw in my face at this point is, *Well Monica, your Mom was married and she was seeing another man. That's not right! She was cheating. She was committing adultery!*

My response to those who feel this way would be; how could I have faulted her? Remember what I mentioned about the intensity of first times? Well, this was the first time I saw her in a relationship that brought a genuine smile to her face. I was rejoicing to see her with a man who wasn't manipulative, controlling, or abusive. She was finally in love with someone who wasn't plotting to control her but allowed her to feel free and smile off years of stress. Her light brought me bliss as I gazed upon her beaming heart. She was shining with love, even though it was under not-so-great circumstances. Had I been older and known what I do today, I would have been able to give her better advice, but I was only seventeen. I only knew that if she was happy, I was happy.

With Ian, I didn't see her as being in a marriage or being a wife. Throughout our lives, I never felt she belonged to him, and she never had. I have no memory of ever seeing them get dressed for a date, a honeymoon, or anything romantic. I never witnessed them share a bottle of wine, celebrate an anniversary, or hold hands in public. I saw him smother her with overly passionate kisses that covered her entire mouth with his moustache. She always looked so uncomfortable, especially when he would grab her or slap her rear in public. That always seemed to embarrass her. "I don't like that, Ian," she would say. She would try to be stern as she avoided his eyes and walked further along.

"Oh, C'mon! You know that's mine anyway," was his smiling response. I never saw them in love. *It simply couldn't be,* I thought. This wasn't love; this was vile. Did she love him, though? I know she did. Yet, it was never easy to love Ian. During one of our car rides, she told me how she believed Ian was her soul mate and during another ride told me, "He brings out the evil in me. I love him, but I can't be with him."

Their love was strange, and by all legal means they were married: not happily, faithfully or lovingly, but on paper, yes, they were husband and wife. However, on paper they could have just as easily been divorced. The paperwork wasn't up to date, and Mom couldn't change it fast enough to keep up with her feelings.

After my grounding was over, I kept the same distance

from Ian. I had just completed my driving course a couple of weeks earlier and had been issued my permit. Needless to say, I wanted to start driving right away, anytime, anywhere.

When I would ask Mom to let me drive her prim and polished Pontiac, I was given a big, laughing NO. It was the same laughing response she gave Junior when he'd badger her for it. When that debate reached a dead end, Ian would chime in and take my side. He had a strange way of admiring me when he wanted to. Once, Caleb and I lay on the roof helping Ian hang Christmas decorations when his lighter suddenly slipped from his pocket and started sliding towards the edge. It was aiming for the edge of the roof, seconds from flying right off. I knew this was a special lighter. It was the only one he used. On its shiny silver cover, Mom had engraved something sweet and given it to Ian as a gift, so I didn't want her to be sad if it was broken. I quickly crawled to the ledge and slammed it down with my hand before it was gone. I looked up at Ian and Caleb who were watching the whole thing.

"That's my girl!" Ian laughed, tossing his head back and rubbing his forehead with his palm. Though I seemed to have made him proud, I wasn't flattered.

"Let her drive, she needs to learn," he would urge Mom. "She'll be fine. She can do it." But she didn't budge. Her countless refusals were because she was afraid I would destroy her car and bring it back in an unrecognizable condition. So, Ian decided to teach me himself. The only problem Mom had with that decision was that Ian had an enormous 4X4 Dodge Ram. It was a vehicle better suited for more experienced drivers, but I was so eager to drive that Ian and I convinced her I could do it.

And I did.

On a Saturday, Caleb, Ian and I took the truck out all over the suburbs of Chicago. Still sadly inexperienced, I stopped in the left turning lane on a red light. "Can I turn?" I asked Ian. There were no cars on the road, so I thought it a perfectly reasonable move. That question only triggered Ian. He began shouting at me, calling me all types of degrading names that chucked away any driving confidence I had built up. "*Stupid, blind, dysfunctional, retarded.*" I was used to his belittling ways and his insulting name calling. His efforts were beginning to lose their effect on me since he had been calling me the same names my entire life. I no longer believed his words, but they still angered me.

I contemplated my choices. I could have retorted back and risked having an argument confined in his car; a potentially dangerous situation. I imagined he might slam my head against the steering wheel if I said anything. Mom wasn't around, so there was even less protection. Caleb was in the back seat, but I knew he wouldn't be strong enough to pry Ian off me. Or, I could say nothing, remain silent, and allow him to throw every upsetting name at me.

Given the limited options, I decided it was a smart decision to keep quiet. *Just let him believe he's right.* It seemed to be the same tactic Mom used. As he shouted, I took the road as a good distraction and avoided making eye contact with him. All I noticed was how his mask was disappearing, faster and faster. He was having less desire to hold it together and slipping more and more easily into rage.

His rapidly changing moods always came as a surprise to me. I never knew what to expect and continually failed to understand his triggers. Sometimes it seemed to be everything.

Other times it seemed to be nothing.

Moments that I perceived as enjoyable were suddenly transformed to chaos. He had an incredible talent to take a beautiful day and turn it into the worst memory. When I thought we were getting along, he would spark a fire and strike away any smile or good feelings I had. He was an equation I'd been trying to solve my entire life, but after years of his destruction, I no longer cared if I failed his tests. I was growing incredibly drained. Dealing with him was a chore I no longer cared to do or even had the energy to try handling. I simply couldn't fake it anymore.

Needless to say, I never asked him to take me driving again. Thankfully, Mom came around and took me herself.

...

Ian's mother was in a wildly confusing world of dementia. I sadly didn't pity her because of the years of ill will she had directed towards me. Some days she had no idea where she was, nor did she remember any of us, not even her grandchildren, or Ian, her son. I saw her trigger Ian's wild eyes as she hung up the phone on him one day after calmly saying, "No, I don't have a son."

Caleb and I awoke for school one morning and we were pouring our cereal in the kitchen when she started stirring from her bed. Grandma usually only got up when it was time to take her medication, but today she decided this wasn't her home and she was leaving.

She started staggering down the stairs, making her way to the front door. Caleb and I tried to calmly steer her back to bed, but she didn't know who we were. She persistently continued to repeat, "I'm going home. I want to go home." Caleb and I stood in front of her, adding to her frustration. With the cup of water in her hand, she held it straight out and tilted it just a little and squinted her eyes tight. Pouring water all over the floor didn't seem like much of a threat, so Caleb and I erupted in laughter, confused how this would get her what she wanted.

After a pointless conversation confirming to her this was her home, she eventually gave up on her pursuit. She hobbled back up the stairs and both of us laughed in relief. We headed off to school, already late.

We all quickly learned that Grandma required twenty-four/seven security detailing which only added to the stressful, complicated dynamics of the home. Ian told us she could never be left alone. Though none of us wanted to take on that responsibility, none of us said no either.

As I handed her Tuesday's medications out of the organizer, I stared at her thin wrinkled cheeks and wispy brown hair as she threw the several pills into her mouth. I handed her the glass of water in my hand, and as she took one large gulp, I wondered what she could have possibly done to raise such an awful person. It must have meant that she, too, was an awful human being. She turned over and covered herself under the sheets. I slowly pulled the door shut and left her alone in the light of day. I didn't know, but I guessed as much had to be true.

. . .

Spring 2009

In the months that followed, I saw Mom's heart filling with love for Evan. They were cute. Though I enjoyed seeing Mom happy, I knew she was swimming in dangerous waters. To avoid any discovery about their relationship, Mom kept Evan's name under a female alias in her phone, *Jen*. She would stay late at work some days to spend extra time with Evan. She spoke about plans for their future which told me they were serious this time. Apparently, they had been looking at homes and were almost set on one. I hadn't seen it yet, but Mom was planning to take me to see it soon.

Like Caleb and I, Mom withdrew from Ian. She barely pretended to care anymore. I never thought Ian was an empty-headed person. In fact, I thought he was deceptively smart. And if we weren't playing our roles, he sensed something was wrong.

Mom was doing her makeup in the bathroom before work. I had just gotten into bed when I heard Ian enter the bathroom and begin talking to her. He sounded casual, sweet and concerned. As I listened closely from my bed below their feet, I heard him asking her about their relationship, their intimacy and their love.

"Do you love me or not?" he asked kindly.

When she intentionally responded with "I don't know" he began to stir. I felt the familiar feeling of rising tension and my hand automatically began reaching for my phone ready to dial 911.

"Yes or no. Do you love me or not?" he asked again. The kindness was leaving his tone. Mom left the bathroom. She had to leave for work soon, but he seemed to be following behind her every step.

"It's a simple question. Do you love me or not?"

"I don't know, Ian. We've gone through a lot." She was trying to be sweet and calm, but none of it was working to her advantage.

"Okay, so do you love me or not?" He wanted an answer right then and there, but her silence kept him unsettled, "Do you love me or NOT?"

He must have asked her twenty times because as I was listening to them, I became annoyed thinking *Mom! Just tell him you don't love him! Just tell him already!*

I came from my room and sat at the top of stairs, looking into the garage through the side door. Mom's car had been running and I could smell the fumes beginning to seep into the house. Ian had undying persistence. She pressed the button to the garage door, and as the loud metal slowly scraped the tracks to relieve the fumes, Ian walked right in front of her car. It was ten minutes past the usual time she left and her pressured tone said she was growing annoyed. She stood behind her driver door in her red jacket and name badge shouting at him to move.

"What are you doing? You're gonna make me late for work! Ian, I need to go!" she shouted.

"Okay, you can go. Just answer my question," he said sarcastically.

"Ian you..."

He interrupted, "Answer my question! Do you love me or not!"

I sat watching their argument fly in circles as he badgered her with the same question over and over. I looked over my shoulder at the microwave clock that said Mom was now thirty minutes late. I knew she wouldn't be stopping for her regular coffee at Dunkin Donuts which may have only made her angrier.

She seemed to have reached her limit because she got in her car and sped off past Ian, leaving him without the answer he was looking for. He stood there in the garage, looking out into the street.

I was certain I didn't want to be in the path of his hostility, so I scurried back to my room before he saw me.

He said nothing. He made no sound. He simply closed the garage door, turned off the light, and quietly went downstairs to saturate the air in cigarette smoke. I lay in bed, replaying their argument in my head.

The next morning during a car ride with Mom, we got on the topic of their dispute. I couldn't think of any reason why she didn't just relieve all the stress they both seemed to be having with the truth and finally tell him, *No, I don't love you anymore!* If we ever wanted him to move on, I believed he needed to hear those words.

The truth had become apparent in the short time since we moved back. All I thought she needed to do was be honest with Ian for the first time ever and it would be the last step in finally letting this all go.

"Mom, why didn't you just tell him? He asked you a million times, why didn't you just tell him?" I asked.

Sitting there in the driver's seat, her voice grew quiet and a somber expression came to her face as she gazed at the road ahead, "Oh. No, honey. You can't do that." She smiled sadly. The worry in her voice kept me silent. I sat, trying to understand what she meant. *Why? Why couldn't she simply end all of this by telling him the truth?* He deserved to know. And we deserved to move on. Yet, in her short, simple words she illuminated a deeper meaning, one I had gravely overlooked.

Her relationship with Ian confused the innocence in me. She appeared to understand something I didn't. Something about Ian I was blind to. Somewhere, in Ian, something existed much deeper than I ever knew, but Mom seemed to be well aware of it.

...

Sunday

May 2009

CHURCH BELLS, off-key choir ensembles, repeated standing, and long, confusing sermons I had no enthusiasm for were not on the top of my weekend priority list. However, Mom made it clear, "That's your problem, too bad. Now, up!" She badgered me out of bed, each time with less patience, and repeatedly told me to, "Get dressed, get dressed" and "Get dressed already!" It was understood that if I was going, Caleb was going, too. So, when I plopped out of bed, so did he. Eventually.

When Caleb and I finished brushing our teeth and dressing ourselves, we went to the kitchen and ate the pancakes Mom had made. I took my two and Caleb took the other twenty-eight. When finished, Mom huddled us up and out the door. I stood outside Mom's car on the driveway under the sun that was radiating through the bluest sky imaginable and scattered clouds. The air was warm, but cool breezes relieved the heavy heat. I could smell the fresh cut grass and flower petals as they drifted through the air.

Ian was working on his car with the garage door open. Mom politely asked, "Do you want to come?" but he ignored her and said nothing. He stood there, calmly wiping his tools clean. She asked again but didn't wait long for him to respond.

"C'mon," she told us, her patience thinning. We got in the car, the hot leather seats burning my skin, and waited a minute longer, possibly to see if he would change his mind. Getting settled in the back seat, I paused to admire Mom's hair through my sunglasses. The sun was directly ahead of us, simply illuminating all her beauty. It was a vibrant, enticing red and it remained so even when I took off my sunglasses for a better look.

"Mom, your hair looks awesome!" I said, watching her confidence shine through her smile.

"Yeah, Mom, you look hot!" Caleb added, now seeing what I was seeing.

"I do!?" she said surprised, enthused, and joking all at the same time. She was wearing a captivating black blouse, jeans that hugged her curves, and black and white heels that always gave her the extra height she needed to be taller than Caleb. She was as radiant as the sun.

"Yeah, Mom, you look gorgeous!" She really looked fantastic.

"You guys, thank you," she said sweetly and drove off.

We arrived at church a little late and took our regular seats in the pews. The service went as usual, never being as daunting as I would predict it to be and always becoming a peaceful family time. After the "and also with you" salutation, the church let out, and we greeted the familiar faces and shook the familiar hands as we made our way back to the car.

A sense of restoration always seemed to embody Mom when we left service. She tried to make this newfound peace last for as long as possible. She was always noticeably in better spirits, as if all her worries had been wiped away, and she was given a clean slate.

We stopped by the Dunkin Donuts for our usual after-church frappes and blueberry cake donuts. Once in hand, we talked and laughed over slurps of deliciousness in the car. I gazed out the window sipping my frappe, then looked at my silent phone to see that Jim was calling. When I answered, he asked what I was up to and if I wanted to come over. Of course, I always wanted to. I quickly asked Mom, and she agreed to take me to his house. With giddy feelings flushing around and instantly forgetting anyone was around me, I said, "I'll see you soon. I love you, too." I immediately froze when I heard the words aloud. Mom's gasp reminded me I had never said those words in her presence before.

"What did you say?" she asked, struck with happy curiosity.

"I do love him, Mom," I said smiling with embarrassment, but relieved as butterflies swarmed in. "I do."

She stared into the road. "Well. Oh. Okay," she replied as she pondered about what I had just said. She sat quiet but smiling.

"I really want you to meet his Mom. I think you would like her a lot." She and Mom both had a deep passion for beautiful tropical weather that I imagined would ignite a great friendship. That, and they were both incredibly sweet.

When we pulled up to Jim's house, he sent me a text saying that his mother was cleaning and not really presentable for a first-time impression.

"Well, that's okay I'll meet her next time," Mom said. "I love you. Call me if you need a ride back."

"Okay, love you too!" I leaned into the driver window, kissed her goodbye and with pouring excitement, rushed up the front porch stairs to see Jim. Mom drove off waving.

...

With Jim, I could have spent hours and never noticed that time had gotten away from us. What seemed like minutes were hours flown by. We both shared a strong passion for music, specifically heavy rock and punk music, so we spent our time showing each other new jams and finding the latest ones we thought just killed it. He was a talented musician who could enchant me with a single strum on one of his many electric guitars. Truly, he was my teenage dream.

The time had passed quickly before I finally checked my phone. When I did, the tiniest alarm echoed within me. There was nothing. There were no missed calls, no text messages, and no voicemails. No one had attempted to reach me, which I found odd seeing that tomorrow was a school day. It had been several hours since I had left, and my time was always hawked when I was allowed out. I was always given a curfew, and an early one at that. I thought today had been a rare opportunity, even a blessing, to stay a while longer and to enjoy my time with Jim.

But my feelings stirred, and I asked Jim to take me home. I suspected that maybe they were testing me to see if and when I would come home on my own. Maybe they had given me a curfew, but I forgot.

Still, I remembered I had two last finals to take the next day for my Art and Literature class, which I still needed to study for.

It was near the end of my Junior year, and with summer so close, I didn't want to ruin my opportunity for summer adventures with Jim. I had spent all day with Jim anyway, so I knew it was time to go home.

After a three-minute drive, Jim and I pulled up to my driveway and exchanged goodbyes for much too long and with too many affectionate embraces. After I entered in the code on the garage key pad, I walked backwards waving goodbye as he drove off. I was a giddy school girl.

I went into the garage and inside the house through the entry door. I opened the door to a warm sunlit room; dusk was beginning to come. Once inside, I took a look around the house to see if anyone was home since I thought it peculiar no one had called me.

After affirming I was alone and off the hook, I went downstairs to my room and began studying for my finals. I spread the books out on my bed and began reading over my material when a knock at the door disrupted my concentration. I went upstairs and realized I had locked the door to the garage. When I opened it, Caleb stood there, holding a familiar bag. He looked oddly confused. "Why is Mom's purse here?" he asked. He held the purse in his hand and pointed to where it had lain on the dirty, concrete floor.

"Oh. I don't know," I answered. I was caught off guard and peered into the garage and looked around.

"And her shoes?" he asked. His concern rose as he pointed to the back of the garage wall at the black and white heels

Mom had been wearing that morning.

"I don't know. I didn't even know they were there." I realized my infatuated eyes for Jim left me entirely unobservant to her things lying on the filthy floor.

Caleb came inside and began looking around. I decided I too should take another, closer scan of the house, in case there was something else I had overlooked.

I went to the kitchen and saw there was uncovered food left on the stove. The lights were also left on and Grandma was asleep lying in her room. No one else seemed to be home.

Caleb called for my attention to the downstairs living room. "These weren't here!" he said. "I left these in Mom's trunk." He pointed to his school belongings which he had cleaned from his locker and placed in her trunk just days ago. I hadn't noticed those on the floor, either. Unsettling feelings began to slip in as we noticed the things that were out of place. Her car was gone.

"I'm calling Mom." Caleb rushed to his phone. I continued to search the house, the rooms, the windows, the dogs. Nothing was stolen or broken. There was no sign of a break in.

"Did she answer?" I exclaimed.

"No, it's going to voicemail." Caleb was becoming upset.

"I'll try calling." The phone rang once and went straight to her voicemail. I tried again and the same thing happened. I tried once more. Same thing. I tried calling her over and over again, and was becoming frantic, "Why isn't she answering?"

Caleb was trying, but with the same spiraling frustration. "I'm gonna call Ian," he said.

"Okay, I'll call him, too." The same dead-end ringing was

shouting in my ear. "What! Ugggh! C'mon! Answer already!" But no one did. I tried calling Ian, then tried calling Mom. Then Ian, then Mom. Again Ian, and again Mom. Very quickly, an hour had flown by with not a single answered call from either of them. The warm glow of the sun was beginning to set on everything.

We tried hopelessly for the next couple of hours, pacing in distressed circles outside on the driveway with no single call having gone through yet. My alarm was now louder.

"Okay, I'm gonna call Jim and just ask him if he can come back." I was confused. I didn't know what to tell him. I needed help, and I needed his clarity. I was beginning to lose focus.

"Jim? Hi, can you come back?" He was as confused as I was, "Yeah, I just want you to come back because my Mom's things are here, but she's not here. Can you just come back?" Without many questions, he said he was on his way.

I immediately hung up with him and called Mom's work in what I knew was an unlikely chance that she went in early. Really early. I got a receptionist that told me she wasn't there. *Evan! I'll call Evan!* When Evan answered, he was at work. "Mom's not home and she's not answering her phone. I was wondering if she might be with you or...?", I gave him what little information I had.

His words summoned the feelings I was so strongly trying to ignore, "Monica, I don't have a good feeling about this."

My heart started sprinting, my words became disoriented and chaos was swarming my breath. Caleb and I locked up the doors, went inside, and stood at the front screen glass door just waiting for someone to come home.

With relentless persistence, we kept calling. Calling, and

calling.

I was pacing in the kitchen, when Caleb's voice grabbed my attention. "Where is Mom?" he yelled as he locked the glass door. I leaped off the stairs, rushing to the door to see who he was talking to. Ian was standing there on the steps, shaken.

"Where is Mom?" Caleb shouted. He had the most serious look in his eyes, and he was demanding Ian answer, "Where is Mom?"

Ian's behavior was entirely unrecognizable. I'd never seen him like this before. He wasn't threatening us nor losing his temper. Instead, he was shaking and answering our questions but wouldn't look directly at us. What was most alarming to me was the wild look in his shifting eyes.

"I don't know!" he answered. "I don't know!"

"Where is Mom?" Caleb was firm with no intention of budging, which made me incredibly uncomfortable, especially since we were refusing to let Ian inside. As Caleb continued to question Ian, I saw Jim pull up on the street behind him. I needed to relieve the tension piling in the doorway, so I unlocked the door, rushed outside past Ian and ran to Jim's car.

"What's going on?" Jim asked.

"I don't know. He's acting weird." I felt safer with Jim present. Caleb came out moments later. We stood with Jim outside his car as the panic in our voices rose.

As the three of us gathered in dispute, we hushed as Ian casually approached us with a calm suggestion. "Maybe she's at Stephanie's house. Why don't you guys check there?" he said, tucking his hands in his pockets.

As I looked up at him, I noticed his eyes never met mine. He looked onto the street, into the trees, into the sky. He looked over me and past me, but never at me.

With hesitation, Caleb and I got into Jim's car and drove off with Ian standing at the street. With Caleb in the backseat, we headed towards Stephanie's house. She was a friend Mom often visited for a drink, but Ian's suggestion spoke a different truth.

"Which way?" Jim asked.

"Turn here!" Caleb answered. I sat in the passenger seat frozen, starring at the ground. My spiraling thoughts had momentarily taken over my ability to speak.

"Monica, which way?"

I tried desperately to make sense of what was happening. None of it felt right. There was a horrible voice whispering Evan's words.

"This is stupid," I blurted out as I interrupted Caleb.

"What?!" he asked.

"This is stupid. She's not at Stephanie's house." I was coming to realize that Ian had never, ever so carelessly suggested I go anywhere. It felt like distraction. It felt like a trick.

"Turn around!" I yelled.

"Where are we going?" Jim asked. His voice was growing worried.

"We need to go back to the house," Caleb said. "I need my charger." He persistently continued to call Mom, and I felt paralyzed with uncertainty. I withdrew into my mind as we drove back to the house.

Sitting in Jim's car, I waited for Caleb to return with his charger. Storms of chaotic thoughts were flooding my head as I tried to summon an answer. *Where is Mom!* Silently, I panicked under my skin, trying not to frighten anyone.

Caleb ran back to the car, "He's in the shower!"

"What!" I shrieked.

"He's in the shower," Caleb repeated.

I was shaking with a kind of fear I'd never known, and Jim could see the worry overtaking me. "Listen, you guys just come to my house and I'll let my parents know what's going on," Jim said.

"Okay."

We arrived at Jim's house and I explained to his parents what was happening. With the little information I could give, they immediately went for the phone and called the police.

"I think they usually have to wait twenty-four hours to report a missing person" they said, guessing that there might be nothing we could do tonight. When I heard the words *missing person* being identified with Mom, numbness started to infect me.

A deep blue hue set on the homes of the peaceful suburb and on the soft blowing leaves of every tree. With the darkness inching closer, I sat on Jim's couch and sank into helplessness while his mother called 911 from the other room.

After a few minutes, she came back, "They're on their way." *My god, what's happening?* I took the short seconds I had to call my tias and tell them what was going on.

A moment later, a knock at the door caught our attention. "I got to go Titi, the police are here now." I hung up the phone. Thankfully, the police department was within ten second's walking distance of Jim's house.

I jolted off the couch to see two officers at the steps and their squad cars at the street. Caleb and I stepped outside, answered their questions and made it clear, "Something is wrong."

They could see we were panicked, but they remained calm and unfazed by our worry. They suggested we go with them to their vehicle and back to the house so they could speak with Ian.

As Caleb and I took the short trip back to our house, every second was filling me with apprehension. I sat enraged as the officers casually asked questions I had no energy to respond to.

When we pulled up to our driveway, Caleb and I stayed with one officer in the car while the other went to the door to talk with Ian. Caleb was right, Ian had showered. I noticed his thin, gray hair was combed back and he was dressed in different clothes. Carefully, I studied his face as he spoke with the officer. He was calm, smiling even. He was not shaking; nothing like he had been just moments ago.

As I peered through the police window at Ian, I realized I'd seen that exact face before. I had come to know it so well. I had been fooled by it all my life and had come to hate it.

It was his mask. It was the same mask he wore to charm us while he was in prison. It was the same mask he was using on the officer. I saw the outstanding actor he was striving to be as he stood there answering the officer ever so politely. He knew something. He had to.

As we waited, the officer stepped outside the vehicle and paced. He leaned in over the window, looking at his partner at the door, "Maybe she just went out for a drink or something." His effort to defuse my panic only infuriated me.

A few moments of conversation seemed to end calmly when the officer came back to the car and opened our door gesturing for us to come out.

"Everything seems fine here. She should be back soon," the

officer told us.

"Thank you, officer!" Ian replied as Caleb and I walked speechlessly back into the house. Ian closed the door and stood hunched, peeking out the window. I watched the officers sitting in their car, stalling for a moment longer. *Please don't leave, please.* I was scared and disgusted by Ian's ability to charm them so effortlessly. Under his breath Caleb murmured, "I just want Mom back."

Ian, still peering out the window, had a savage look in his eyes. He spoke to us with rigid sarcasm. "Yeah, me too," he snarled. After an unusually long moment, I watched as our only help disappeared off the driveway and trapped us in Ian's grasp. Ian was dripping with instability, and I felt the danger of dark clouds lurking over our home.

I darted to my bedroom as Caleb stayed there, arguing with Ian at the top of the steps. I called Jim back, frantically begging him to return and in a rage because the police had left us!

Caleb bolted into my room a moment later and locked the door. "What are we gonna do?" he asked. He looked worried, and I wanted to have an answer for him.

"I don't know! I don't know!" I answered. I tried to focus on all the thoughts bouncing off the walls of my mind; *We could sneak out the window, but where would we go? Should I pack a bag? What are we doing? We have to do something! What am I doing? Where is Mom?*

In those uncertain minutes, I had been ignoring my phone. When I checked it, I saw I had multiple missed calls from my tias and Junior. When Junior answered the phone, he said, "Hey, we're on our way over." *Thank God!* I had the smallest relief.

"Okay. We're in my room. The police just left. How long are you gonna be?" I asked.

"We'll be there any minute. Just stay there," he assured me.

As Caleb and I paced in the echoing silence, we brainstormed about every clue thus far. The hope of finding Mom was proving useless. Ian's award-winning performance had convinced me he was responsible for Mom's disappearance.

Junior arrived with my Tia Carlita near nightfall, and they brought police with them. I left the house while Ian was speaking with different police officers and came to hear there was a different problem. Standing in the driveway, Ian argued with the officers about Caleb; he wouldn't let him leave. I stood close by, listening with my Tia.

"Monica, she can go, but Caleb, he's my son. He's staying with me," Ian said as he paced, and I knew this man. I knew his persistence would be unfailing. And it was. He appeared like a caged animal up against the wall. He stepped aside to make a phone call and all I could hear from his stern tone was, "I need you here, Jay. I need you here." I sensed he was dangling on the edge of his mask.

Realizing this was starting to take longer than expected, I sat with Junior in their car while the officers attempted to reason with Ian to let Caleb leave. Pacing back and forth, smoking cigarette after cigarette, Ian argued with the officers trying to withstand their efforts.

As I was attempting to make out what they were saying, I was also getting Junior up to speed on what had happened thus far. My nerves were like lightning shooting through my veins. I felt sick. I didn't want to leave Caleb alone with Ian.

Time crept into the later hours of darkness; there was still no sight of Mom. No call had been returned and worry had grown like a virus in all of us. As Ian continued to refuse to let Caleb go, the street began flooding with our family members and police lights were flashing through the neighborhood. The last time I recall the streets flooded with these kinds of worried faces and flashing lights was the night Mom ran out the front door after Ian had shot her. Gazing through the faces in the quickly filling street of our neighborhood, I feared what it meant for us now.

All of my closest family members were there, waiting. Thankfully, my Tio bravely pleaded with Ian to let Caleb leave in sincere and careful words.

Ian avoided Tio's eyes in the same way he had avoided mine. Tio was light, trying not to make this appear to be the bigger situation it really was. As he continued to press against Ian's resistance, a familiar face came out of the darkness. It was the friend Ian had called, Jay. He was probably the only one I had ever met whom Ian had worked with as a police officer. He was a man I remember vaguely seeing as a child. But, I was puzzled. I remembered Jay had lived all the way on the other side of town and couldn't help but wonder just how he had arrived here with such impeccable timing.

When Ian saw Jay, they stepped aside to speak. I will never know whose words convinced Ian or why he was convinced at all, but shortly after they spoke, Ian agreed to let Caleb leave.

Caleb ran from the house and rushed into a car with my tia. I leapt into a different one with Junior and everyone immediately dispersed. It was all over so suddenly.

At an empty nearby gas station, we all met up. Everyone

parked and huddled together under the blaring, white station lights. As my family stood together exchanging thoughts on what to do and just trying to make sense of what was happening, my mind had run off. I could not bring it back. I was numb. I heard nothing they said.

"Are you okay?" my tia asked, looking sadly upon me.

"Oh yeah, yeah, I'm fine," I responded on auto-pilot, having not yet understood how the day had brought me to this gas station when just a few hours earlier I had been exchanging smiles with Jim.

Dazed and confused, I looked around at the dark streets. It was after 11:00 PM with barely any cars in sight. Frayed with worry and hopeless feelings, my family decided to take Caleb and me to my tia's home to rest for the night. During the drive, Caleb and I sat in the backseat silently soaking in our wasted emotions as my tio tried to spark distracting conversation. I sat silently, drowning in questions and watching the bright orange street lights flash through the car, casting shadows around me. I stared at the shadows, trying to see Mom's face.

Where is Mom? Where is she?

. . .

Arroyo

WHETHER IT WAS BECAUSE of my instinctive desire to move towards happiness or because of my own perceived responsibility to take care of others, I woke up the next morning with a positive mind. Overall, I was calm.

The night in my aunt's downstairs living room was quiet and undisturbed. Yet, I felt as if I hadn't rested. Caleb and I woke hopeful that answers awaited us, but soon after starting the day, it appeared there were none. My tia and tio had already left to speak with the police.

All morning, I paced in silence and barely ate. I didn't know anything yet and I wasn't going to assume anything either; this made it easier to stay calm.

In my deepest heart of hearts, I felt as if I knew what was about to happen. I thought the harder I wished for it, the more likely it was to happen. Somehow, I had the emotional power to summon my own destiny. I believed that by channeling my thoughts, my emotions, and my heart, I could control my own outcome.

I saw no other life that could possibly exist for me without Mom. I believed that if I could see no other life, then no other life existed. If no other outcome made sense, then no other outcome could be possible. Period. So, I took peace in knowing she was going to come back to me, because with all the forces of the cosmos I believed that she would.

Night started to fall and I was losing patience. Consumed with anguish, I spiraled in thought wondering, *why in the hell have all the adults been gone all day! Why hasn't anyone given us any answers yet!* There had been little communication from anyone. I knew they were busy, but as nine o'clock turned into ten I felt I was going to explode. I lingered around the basement, itching in agitation, trying to watch a movie or a show, play a game or go online; anything to distract me.

At last, hours into the night, my cousin announced they were on their way back. I was quiet, sitting in the basement with Caleb, waiting just a few more painful minutes when I heard the loud garage door opening. I jumped out of my seat.

Above me, I heard them all rustling through the doors and come creaking down the stairs. Caleb and I stood to meet them, and my tio placed his hand on my shoulder and walked me back to the sofa. Caleb and I sat surrounded by my family and my tia knelt down in front of us. As I began to panic, she looked at us, already fighting back tears. She hadn't said a word yet, and tears already began to fill their eyes. "Your Mom, she's..." she could barely speak the words... "she's gone."

Control was lost. The earsplitting cry our voices emitted was unrecognizable. I was unrecognizable. In that hideous moment, we became two children without a mother. Devastation consumed us. Shouting. Screaming. Ripping into the high heavens with my raw, deafening cries. Every awful, unimaginable emotion within the universe demolished me. Agony. Excruciating pain shattered my muscles. My family held me close. I was no longer Monica, but a daughter now deeply, deeply wounded.

Time has allowed me to eliminate the events that followed. I don't want to remember it all. But the feeling of loss, the transformation of thoughts from being with to being without and processing the reality into what it means to no longer have someone in your life you deeply love, is a feeling forever scarred within me.

...

For the next several weeks, I was functioning like a used rag tossed in the corner. Every morning the torturous reality returned, forcing me to live it all over again. I was a desolate, barely operable, capsule of a person. Nothing, truly nothing, existed within me. My senses stopped and my orientation left. I became a void. It was as if I had fallen into my own black hole and was being crushed onto myself. Numbness corroded everything, and no thoughts could form other than those of Mom. Unrecognizable and devastated, I was forced to call this my life.

Overhearing family discuss the details was unbearable. I could not hear a single, solitary word about any of it. Not yet. Nor did I want anyone to ask, *how are you doing? Are you hungry?* Or to ramble out the useless words, *how could this happen?* I couldn't so much as mention Mom's name, let alone hear it. Simple words were already more than I could handle.

While existing in emptiness, all my observant tendencies

had abandoned me. I didn't notice that I hadn't showered and had been wearing the same clothes for the past three days. My uncle kindly suggested getting me out of the house for a while to buy some clothes. Everything I owned was still at that house and for the past couple of days I had entirely forgotten I had none of my belongings with me. He took me to Kohl's, and with a blind mind, I wandered the aisles of happy, flowery summer clothing.

With a kind attempt to take my mind to better places, my tio made jokes about wearing the clothes himself and about how good the floral dresses might fit him. I smiled automatically and continued my hazy search, not even sure what I was looking for. I put some shirts and shorts in the cart and left. When we arrived back to my aunt's house, I went downstairs to the dark living room and admired my new things for a moment. A smile came across my face. My admiration was quickly met with the thought, *I should call Mom and tell her what I got.* I reached for my phone and my hand froze just inches away from it. I stared, paralyzed, as reality surprised me and settled in deeper. There was no one to call. I slowly crippled myself to the floor and laid my face in my hands as knots swelled in my throat and my eyes locked themselves into darkness. *She's gone.* I sat on the miserable thought for hours before someone shouted from the top if the stairs, "Monica, are you down there?"

I quietly swallowed my pain before speaking. "Monica! Sweetie, are you down there?" they shouted again.

"Yeah!" I said, grabbing hold of myself. "I'm here."

Truly, I wasn't.

...

As the weather warmed and schools let out for summer vacation, Caleb and I kept isolated inside, sleeping almost all hours of the day. We lay awake in the basement every night, talking for hours and crying for several more over memories of Mom and the pain we felt when her memory seemed to bring her to life. We had no indication of morning. Thick blankets and curtains covered the windows. When we woke, tears were already waiting to emerge again.

I couldn't fathom it, couldn't process exactly what this meant: Mom was gone. With every passing moment, I was taken further and further away from her, allowing me less and less time to change what had happened. Somehow, I had left her behind *in* that day. My deepest, strongest instinct was telling me to *GO BACK! Go back for her!* And my rational mind said, *Go where, Monica?* I desperately imagined the possibility to go back in time and save her. My heart was holding on to the possibility of her return and would for the next few years. I imagined that after the chaos had settled, she would come out of hiding to tell me how this had all been a terribly elaborate plan, but a necessary one, in order to make Ian believe, once and for all, that she was really gone. Vividly, I imagined she would come back to say she was sorry for making me believe this, but it was the only way to leave Ian for good. My mind told me that she loved me, and she would be back soon to relieve my heart from its rotting captivity.

But, there was no going back. Whether I wanted to or not, time continued carrying me forward. As if being drawn away by the current, I desperately wanted to sail back through the storm for her. I hated time, but fighting it was both pointless and effortless.

There came a moment of both comfort and pain days later as Caleb and I lay on my tia's bed listening to the music on her laptop. I clicked any random song and let the quiet playlist soothe us as we slept. When I woke, tears were swarming, and Caleb was lying on my stomach. The song "Halo" by Beyoncé caught my attention. I was reminded of how music had brought Mom and me together. We liked dancing. Once at a stop light, she turned up the volume and we danced to "Forever" by Chris Brown. At home, she tried to show me the moves she had in high school and taught me The Twist. She stuck out her leg, placed her hands on her hips and twisted her dangling foot side to side, along with the sway of her hips. As I listened to the powerful lyrics, my mind decided to cross over and finally take a step into the murky waters. The words

EVERYTHING IS ABOUT TO CHANGE

stamped themselves into my awareness. With Caleb soundly asleep, I whispered the words out loud to myself, "Everything is going to change" and a heavy, sunken feeling came to my chest. Trembling crept into my fingers, and fear rushed through my heart as my ears heard the words aloud for the first time. Everything is going to change. It was the only moment I needed to prove that without Mom, nothing would ever be the same again.

...

There was little time to digest the change of course in our lives. Caleb was graduating eighth grade next week and both his birthday and Mom's birthday were just eight days after that.

It was a celebration we had spent the last thirteen years com-
bining into one. Now, everyone's spirits were crushed. There
was not a sliver of desire for those days to come. We might as
well have been wearing blindfolds, for we plunged through the
days lifelessly. Everyone's mind was on Mom's wake and funeral
ahead.

My tia came downstairs to explain it all to us. There were
so many daunting days ahead. I had to write a speech for the
funeral and I had to consider what I wanted to leave with Mom
in her coffin. My tia asked if I wanted to take part in choosing
the coffin itself and even in choosing Mom's last clothes for the
wake and burial. "What would she want to wear on her last day
gathered with all of us?" she asked. "What looks like her?"

A photo of Mom needed to be chosen so it could be printed on the service cards. The daunting task of looking through
pictures of Mom's beautiful smile horrified me. But that wasn't
even the end of the list. She asked me a question I never thought
I would have to answer: what would her headstone say? It was
something I never once gave any thought to because the idea
was too awful to bear.

As I got older, I still made Mom come to my bedside and
tuck me in. Once, as she was covering me beneath my sheets she
said, "You know, I'm not going to always be here." She smiled
as she spoke to me.

"Mommy! Don't say that," I said, instantly upset and saddened by the thought as I latched on to her belly.

"Well, it's true. Mommy isn't always going to be here,
okay? It happens to everyone." But I ignored her attempt to
discuss it any longer. I never imagined the day would come as
soon as it did.

With all the dreadful decisions to be made, there was one that could be made effortlessly, a decision that took no thought at all. It was the decision to use her maiden name over her married name:

Irma Rosa Arroyo

With withering strength, I wrote my speech and helped pick out a graceful rose gold chest with elegant single stem roses carved out of the corners. I helped choose a shimmering dress that embodied Mom's vibrant style and, as a family, we decided on a photograph. It was her most recent picture and had been taken at the church just weeks before she disappeared.

Leading up to the day of the wake, I prepared myself for what I would see. What I would do. What I would say. It felt like eternity since I'd seen Mom, and I missed her. I desperately wanted my own chance to say goodbye.

When the day came, the white funeral home was overflowing with family. They drove in, flew in and swarmed in from all over the states to share their goodbyes. As more and more people came through the doors with somber faces, my heart began smiling for the first time in days at the sight of the service room quickly converting into standing room only. Love was there. In that room. Love was alive, bursting at the seams. It came from the crowded souls dressed in black who were just trying to find a view of the flowers and Mom's still face. Everyone was noticing what I saw. She was deeply loved.

"She touched all these lives," were the words someone whispered. With all the faces around me, I couldn't even tell who had spoken, but the words allowed everyone to smile and re-

lieve their heavy faces for a brief second. Their presence made me feel all the more appreciative to have a mother like her.

I wandered the service home and greeted family, some of whom I had never met and didn't know I was Irma's daughter. We consoled one another, hugging and kissing freely. All of us were linked in sorrow.

Though it was with the best intentions, *I'm so sorry for your loss* was beginning to get under my skin. The words alone were triggering an angry response. I didn't want reminding. But was there really anything else to say? They couldn't have said anything that was going to ease my pain anyway, so I kindly thanked them, accepted their condolences and continued wandering alone. Had I known it would be heard again for the rest of my life, I may have reacted very differently.

The service began and I sat in the front row with Junior and Caleb listening to every person in the room shed tears for her. I knew many of them were unaware of what had happened in the last days of her life.

My heart shatters even harder when I return to the plans she was making for her life before she left it. She was trying to live, trying to rid herself of an evil man and years of torment. During the years of Ian's imprisonment, she had come to embrace life differently in a way that opened her up to the exciting and beautiful parts of it. Her growth allowed her to shift towards a life without violence. Leaving Ian was the last part in fulfilling her transformation, and my deepest pain is that she never got to live a life that was ever free of him.

I was thankful for Evan. He had helped her find happiness that she had long, long forgotten. He had helped her spend time understanding what a civil relationship could be like, and that you could have a life you actually enjoyed. You could make plans, book a ticket, and travel without asking for anyone's approval. You could have a relationship without manipulation, fear, or violence. You could spend unconditional love on someone and have it genuinely returned. You could use your hard-earned money on yourself, give attention to your needs, love yourself, care for yourself and find strength in yourself. You could manage a home and three wild children. You could be independent and survive without your abuser. You could do all the things he said you couldn't. You could become more confidently capable of yourself and be surrounded by people who loved you. You could be yourself, completely, and receive love in return for nothing other than love. Yes, you could.

She saw this.

If not for someone else's senseless evil, she would have lived it. She was moving toward it with impeccable speed and I, thrilled to see her embracing it, was so proud of her.

It was the first wake I had ever attended, and the last one I ever wanted to. Though I tried to appear strong and well-composed because I didn't want the attention of people seeing me cry, inside I wanted to erupt. I ached through it all but couldn't allow myself to release any of it.

In front of every withered face, the words I had prepared were spoken into life. Caleb stood by my side, and I fought back the choking grasp of tears. When I was finished, barely having made it through, Junior stood up to speak from his heart. He hadn't prepared anything, so he gazed at the floor, speaking the short sentences that came to his mind. I was sitting next to Tia, who noticed that Junior's swearing was beginning to bring gasps to the room. Junior always had a bad habit of adding, "and shit" at the end of every sentence, and the habit hadn't gone anywhere. Tia whispered his name as she patted the seat next to her, hoping he would wrap up his speech and take a seat. But my sweet brother only looked at her with tears in his eyes and continued to speak his sadness. It didn't happen then, but years later we all had a good laugh about it.

When the next dreadful day came to say goodbye to her sweet face, I gently pressed my trembling lips to her forehead and left my speech tucked underneath her folded hands. It was the last thing I could ever give her, and it brought me comfort to know she would be the only one to remember my words forever.

The only person who hadn't shown their face in the last several weeks or made any attempt to help or send condolences was Ian. At one point during the emotional events of the wake, he was spotted lingering across the street of the funeral home. Whenever one of my family members saw him, they made sure he knew he was not welcome and with the help of the men in our family, they all chased him off. They were baffled and angry that he had the nerve to even show his face. I, on the other hand, was not surprised. In spite of the horrific tragedy he had just brought upon this family, I knew he would still attempt to attend her service and try to see her. Truthfully, until that instant, I had forgotten he still existed. In my heart, Ian had died that night, too.

Regrettably, Ian was still able to continue his life while the dozens of crying eyes gently laid our loving mother, daughter, sister, tia and friend to rest in peace.

Legally, it was too early to make a case. Nothing had moved forward yet. Investigators and special teams were still analyzing our garage for evidence, still retracing the events of that day and the days leading up to it. There was no guarantee a case could even be made. There was no guarantee there was even anything they could do.

Without any ability to help, our family had to wait and place our every ounce of faith in them. We were hoping, praying, and wishing they would find enough to convict the only person we suspected.

...

In the days to come, I would find myself both numb and unfathomably emotional at the same time. I had slept more in the last few days than I had during my entire school year, yet still felt drained and motionless. I would eventually cry past the point of tears and slide into fits of rage. I would have no appetite for days and came to resent sleep because it was only a moment's pause from grief. The loss of my mother would bring me the most confusing and strangest of emotional experiences I would ever feel.

No matter that the hardest days were behind us, they were still weighing heavily on our hearts and minds. We had spent the summertime in slow grief, but time was still carrying me forward, taking me further away from Mom. I had little strength to handle the additional chaos that began to surface.

Hesitantly, I sat down with my tias, tios, brothers and father one Sunday after an especially difficult church service to discuss what would become our future living arrangements. It was something I hadn't even considered until that day. As the conversation unfolded, it seemed to have already been decided that Caleb and I were going to be separated. Caleb would stay with one of my tias, while Junior and I would move miles away to live with our father.

Though I lividly disagreed, there was nothing else they saw fit and there was nothing I could do. I was seventeen. I couldn't live on my own and wasn't old enough yet to even try. It was not my choice. My helplessness gave me no other option but to comply. It was going to be the first time since he was born that Caleb wouldn't be by my side. We had spent our whole lives making the same memories together. Now, I was losing him, too.

. . .

August 2009
Junior and I moved in with our dad, stepmother, Lydia, younger stepbrother Darien, and younger stepsister Joselyn. For the past several years, my regular weekend visits to Dad's house had long been disrupted. Work was in the way, something came up, and so on. Though they had owned it for years, I had yet to even visit his new house. When I originally had the realization lying in my tia's bed that everything was going to change, I had no idea what it was going to morph into until now.

My father's house was out in the middle of the country; a lifestyle I was entirely unfamiliar with. His house was a new model that he and Lydia designed themselves. It was so new that the other houses in the subdivision were still being built. There were no trees and clean, long stretches of roads lined with storybook cookie-cutter style homes with perfect landscapes and only a local Wal-Mart in the town. For many, isolation is ideal. For me, it felt like I had been exiled. The last thing I wanted to do was entirely isolate myself from the people I could still hold on to.

Dad enrolled me in the local high school where I would start my first year in my last grade as a senior. The only person I would know was going to be my stepbrother Darien who was starting his year as a freshman. For years, I had long been excited to spend a year in school with Caleb. High school was supposed to be the year we would finally have together again since leaving our Baptist school six years ago. But I had to let that go, along with a lot of other plans I had looked forward to. Caleb was going to start a new life at a new school, somewhere in his own middle of nowhere.

I had little to nothing to my name. In order to start buying what I needed like shoes, clothes, school supplies, Dad decided I needed to start working. I interviewed with the manager of a local Panera Bread-type restaurant where Dad worked called Mary's Café. The manager barely said a word to me, and I was hired to be a server. I would be taking orders on a register, preparing trays, serving them, cleaning up and closing down.

I had no desire to work or to breathe the air I was breathing, let alone smile a fake smile to customers. Resentment, anger and millions of other stewing negative emotions began brewing and boiling inside of me.

Every part of this new life was being decided for me and eventually, when routine settled in, it started to look something like this: wake up, sit alone on the bus to school, go through my entire day not saying a word other than *excuse me* or *thank you* to anyone. It was keeping my head down during lunch time, or eating in the bathroom alone, or sometimes not at all. It was finding my bus, taking the same lonely, time-wasting trip home, quickly getting dressed for work, and waiting for Dad or Lydia to drive me forty-five minutes to a job I didn't even want and where the only time I spoke was when someone spoke to me. I was trying to make the best of it, but most days I was crawling out of my own skin, and it all seemed pointless.

The thought of Mom drew me back with every step I took forward. When I finally made it home after work by 10:00 PM, I'd shower, crawl into bed and drown myself in tears on the days that had been hardest, or simply just because I had to. No one knew the heartache I was feeling underneath the pleasant smile and positive cooperation I chose to show them. *I should be grateful,* I thought. *I should be thanking him for even taking me in. Things could be a lot worse, Monica.* But I simply couldn't be grateful, thankful or appreciative in any way for having been erupted from the life I knew for so long. Even if it wasn't the best, this wasn't how I wanted to leave it. I couldn't tell Dad I didn't want the job; it was clear there were no other financial options. I wasn't even sure quitting would have helped anyway.

At the new school, I felt like an alien who just wanted to get back to her home planet. I was surrounded by strangers I had no interest in making friends with. Since it was the last year before everyone would graduate and head off to college, *what's the point?* I avoided everyone's eyes and their attempts to talk with me. I cried to myself in class at the mere thought of being there and how everything had gotten me there in the first place. I wanted it all to be over and was still waiting for Mom to come back to me, to take me back home, and to pick up life where we left it. I missed her deeply. I missed Caleb, my boyfriend, my best friend, my teachers, my privacy, my neighborhood. Even though everyone was doing everything in their power to help me through, I couldn't stand the course my life was taking. Life had chosen me for a game of Tetris and reordered everything I saw as familiar and I loathed how it was stacking itself back up.

On the weekends when there were no obligations, I stayed in bed till 4:00 to 5:00 PM listening to that "Halo" song by Beyoncé and allowed the weight of my emotions to crush me. I thought I could get it all out of me. I thought that if I cried more, eventually I wouldn't have anything left, but sadly, the tears always came. I would lay there in my sister's bed, not yet having brushed my teeth, eaten, or changed my clothes. The bright sun would be blaring into the room after Dad decided to open the curtains in an effort to get me up. I didn't have the strength to close them and remained motionless in misery.

I could not take on other people's emotions when I barely had the strength to take on my own. However, suddenly, I realized I had completely forgotten about a person whose feelings truly did matter to me: Evan. I hadn't spoken to Evan at all since the funeral and immediately wondered how he had been doing after everything he, too, had lost. When I called him later that night, I was shocked at his response. We spoke for no longer than a couple of seconds before he asked that I no longer stay in communication with him. Hurt and confused, I agreed. I hung up the phone and that was the last phone call I ever made to him.

My heart's load was starting to overwhelm me but was lightened when I was finally able to see Jim. He had always brought me happiness, and he stayed by my side, continuing to do so. He would drive the two and a half hours to see me and we would walk at a local park and talk. It was all I had the energy for. Seeing his face made me smile, and for a moment I remembered what it was like to be happy, even though I knew it would be gone as soon as he left. Jim continued to take the drive every other week, but eventually we both grew bored with the lifeless town, and his visits became fewer over the following months.

Thankfully, Dad came up with the idea that maybe I was ready for a car. I could use it to get around, go to school, and go to work. Weeks later, after bringing the idea to my attention and checking out some dealerships, he surprised me with a red Dodge Neon. It was parked in the driveway: a four-door, glossy, little car with red balloons tied all over it.

Dad looked at me with excitement, "What do you think!"

"I love it!" I said softly. I knew my reaction wasn't where it should have been. Inside I really was happy, I just couldn't bring it to my face. I wasted no time before I started taking it everywhere. I drove it to work every day, and on the weekends, made trips back to my hometown to visit Nikki and Jim. I was relieved and empowered to finally have some freedom and the luxurious ability of choice.

...

November 2009

Sometimes I think too much. I couldn't help but have questions about my new car. I knew Dad was on a small budget; he had made that clear when I moved in. Curiously, I considered where the money had come for such a nice, first car. In no way was it the beater I had expected. I took notice of quick, drastic changes happening around me. Dad and Lydia hired painters to splash the main level with a bold rustic orange and red palette. New furniture arrived. The downstairs living room was soon furnished with a new sofa set, matching side tables and a coffee table. There was also a large sturdy wooden desk and a leather chair. The upstairs was revamped with the same matching sofa and new TV. Dad's basement bar had doubled in size, his bar shelves fully stocked with various new bottles of liquor. He even added small round tables and chairs to the lounge area he created near the dance floor. Just a couple months ago, when I had moved in, none of this was there and I couldn't help in wondering, *how?*

I was confused. I was still trying to build my wardrobe back up and had just bought my backpack for school with the money I had worked for. After taking notice for several weeks of all new things filling the home, my curiosity was overblown. I needed to know. I assumed the worst but was hoping to be wrong and re-lieved of my worries, however, I just couldn't allow the elephant to keep standing in the room.

One night, I gathered the audacity to ask Dad exactly how he had the money for all of this. I accepted that I might be en-tirely out of line but felt that was better than being lied to.

"Dad, can I ask you something?" I knew there was no going back now.

"Yeah," he replied, seemingly uninterested.

"How do you have the money for all of this?" As he sat on his new sofa watching his new TV, he let out a large sigh. He lowered the TV volume and began to explore bits and pieces of the truth. "Well, there was some money," he eventually said.

With a few short sentences, he cautiously explained to me that after Mom passed away there had been money intended for her children: Junior, Caleb, and me. But my family, including my father, deceived Junior into signing it over to them. They believed that if Junior remained the beneficiary, the money would be quickly wasted.

Dad said he had placed one part of this money aside in some sort of CD account that accumulates interest over time; nothing I would see for the next fifteen years and nothing that made any sense to me. The other part of the truth was, "Oh well." He did every dance to tip-toe around the question I was asking, "Where did the rest of the money go?"

With my every attempt to ask, he would make every attempt to provide a distant and vague response that didn't make me feel as if I received an answer. The bottom line I received was *oh well* and *too bad* for my losses.

He admitted to having used the money on my new car but wouldn't say a word about having used it on any of their recent lavish expenses. He didn't have to. His avoidance and indirect responses said it all. Whether he was telling me the truth or not, I didn't know, but I felt a part of my trust for him had been lost.

I felt cheated, manipulated, used. Enraged! Fuming! Livid! Not only did it fuel me, knowing I had been lied to, but in our grieving, Junior and Caleb had been lied to as well. My father and family were the people we trusted to pick us up from the worst moment of our lives. They were the family we trusted to comfort us in this time of loss. This was the family who took me in and I suddenly questioned if it was only for the money.

The sight of mom's money having been wastefully and deceitfully used to furnish their home disgusted me. I could no longer stand the sight of my surroundings and the people happily living in them.

...

During a weekend with Jim, I vented to his mother about what was happening back in my middle of nowhere home and the lies that were decorating those walls. I couldn't handle another major life change that wasn't the direct result of my own choice. Her kind heart and comforting words reminded me there were still good people in the world; *I* could still be a good person. I dried my eyes after unloading my distress, thanked her for listening, and returned to Jim's room.

Later that week, I spoke to Jim's mother on the phone, who extended an invitation that changed every helpless bone I thought I was crippled by. They offered their home to me.

I probably gave it less than a whole second's thought, before ecstatically accepting. I couldn't thank them enough and said it a million and two times just to make sure they knew. When I hung up the phone with Jim, I resonated in the happiness that came over me. Without their kindness, I would have continued to drown in the quicksand that was consuming me. Jim's parents had pulled me out.

I wanted to finish the last semester with my class, graduate with my friends, and play the final season with my badminton team. I wanted to go back to my friends, my boyfriend, and my neighborhood. I was sick and tired of everyone making choices for me that left me in a worse place than where I started.

I had no difficulty in telling Dad I had decided to leave. I'd had enough. Dad fought my decision with little effort, "If you feel like you need go then, I guess I can't stop you."

The day after Christmas, Jim and his parents drove the two hours out to no-man's land and helped me load up my small bundle of bags into their SUV. It was bittersweet saying good-bye to Dad, Lydia, and my siblings. I didn't want to leave with these wounds open, but I wasn't ready to forgive him and took advantage of my opportunity to make a fresh start.

With a sense of relief, I joined Jim and his parents in the car and our parents shook hands with little or no words. As I drove off with Jim and his family onto the miles and miles of empty road, I felt a huge weight dropped from my shoulders as I dove into a life I was choosing. This was no longer my home, no longer my school and no longer my job. It was a choice I had made for myself, and I felt it was the beginning of many.

...

Wandering the Unfamiliar

IT WAS TOO SOON. I was too all-about-me and my emotions and not in a place to comprehend anything. I was consumed by my own anger, my resentment, and the frustration about the way things had ended with my family after Mom. To an extent, I believe my anger was valid. I thought I was understandably justified to be resentful about having been cheated, justified to be angered by the deception from everyone. Yet, years later I have adopted a crucial piece of wisdom: just because you're right, doesn't make you right.

Let me explain.

I could have very easily and tightly latched onto all my anger and sat it right next to me like a new best friend. I could have easily decided to carry it in my back pocket everywhere I went. For the rest of my life, I could have allowed it to stand by my side and dictate my every decision not to call Dad for Father's Day, Christmas or any other holiday. I could have allowed my grudges to continue to dominate my decision to isolate my-self from the rest of my family forever, never thinking twice. It would have been tremendously easier to stay angry about the stolen money and struggles I faced as a result of not having it. To stay in the same hostile place for the rest of my life was the obvious route and quite honestly, I took that path for a long time. I couldn't let it go. I was right. They were wrong. It could be seen no other way. Right?

Wrong.

One day I suddenly realized years had passed, years, and I was still carrying that bucket of anger on my head. I was still feeling cheated while everyone had moved on. Nobody cared anymore! They even forgot why we stopped talking in the first place. I didn't! I remembered! I was blinded by my fury and hadn't learned my lesson yet. Years later, the lesson was still there, dangling in front of my face. Life was still waiting for me to *stop whining* and *get over it already! Move on!*

Thankfully, I did.

While you live, you have to learn. You must. If you choose not to learn from the experiences life has given you, you will probably become a very grumpy, lumpy person with a long list of all things horrible that keep happening to you and you just can't understand why. Well, maybe it's because you haven't even completed the first lesson. The lesson waaaay back when. The Step One you decided to skip and forget. You can't go any fur-ther until you do it, learn it, or fix it.

You can effectively develop your character and change your life drastically when you choose to forgive, even when forgive-ness is not deserved. Confusing? Yes. You need to learn to give when everyone else has taken. You need to listen, when everyone else is loud. You need to love, when everyone else is hating. These are the hardest times to do the right thing, and they are the moments when it matters most.

Actually, the most important lessons come during what seems to be the worst possible timing. How else is life going to make you pay attention?

It took a lot of years and a lot of sulking, but I finally chose to forgive everyone who had hurt me. It came as no easy task, but in my heart, I let it go. I wasn't going to remain distant and cold any longer. In that choice, I was released from a spell I didn't know I had put myself under. I could finally allow myself to move forward and onto Step Two.

...

February 2010
Returning back to my old school after the new year made me feel exactly how I hoped it would: relieved. Seeing all of my friends' happily surprised faces when I returned for the first day made me feel like I had made the right choice. To my surprise, Jim, the person I expected it from the most, actually had little reaction to the whole change.

When my birthday came around in February, Jim was lacking in his normal big and bold approach to celebrations. In all of our anniversaries, birthdays and holidays he had always managed to shower me with gifts, surprises and extravagant, thoughtful plans. I never asked for it, but eventually I grew accustomed to it. So when his celebration energy seemed low for my birthday, I took notice, but decided not to think much of it, seeing as a lot had been happening, and we were still adjusting to living life under the same roof.

Days later, when Valentine's Day approached, I grew even more concerned. He made no plans. No surprises. Not even so much as a card. Nada. *Well, all right then.* Jim was being strange and barely spoke a word all day. After having spent the whole unromantic day in my own thoughts, I grew agitated. It was not because I didn't have flowers, candy or a giant stuffed teddy, but because I sensed something was really wrong between us.

That night, when I asked Jim to talk, he gave me the response I was dreading most to hear:

It's over.

Moving in was too much too soon. I was everywhere he turned. He saw me too much. He felt more like friends. I had somehow become like a sister, not a girlfriend and yada, yada, yada.

It was that easy to put me right back into my low, crushed feeling of defeat. There was no winning. I couldn't be happy living with my father in the corn fields, and I couldn't be happy here with Jim. Where on this planet was I supposed to go? I had no idea which direction my life's ship was supposed to be sailing. More than anything, I now felt like a giant waste of space intruding into my boyfriend's home.

For the next several nights I cried for three reasons: Mom, Jim, and myself. Every wall seemed just perfect to slam my head into. How could I have been so incredibly stupid thinking other people would solve all my problems? This was my first mistake. Without realizing it, I was behaving like the same passive, compliant child I'd grown up to be, waiting for someone else to give me the green light. I had always waited for directions or opinions from someone who I assumed to be a smarter person than I was. Rolling over into a fetal position, I just prayed someone would give me the answers to my own life. I gave up.

This is not the way life works. Not even in the slightest. In fact, nothing will happen for someone with this kind of pitiful, woe-is-me approach. Perhaps we do this because we want everything to be handed to us. Or at the very least, we're willing to try and see if someone will act first before we do anything for ourselves. It's silly. The universe doesn't respond to pity with reward. It will simply frown on you. This was my second adult lesson.

I despised the pitiful, pathetic person I had become. I blamed everything wrong in my life on the universe and cried out the question, *why me?* I wanted to give up and live as the careless, drug-using, prostituting, angry lowlife everyone was expecting me to become. It's true, the worst sequence of events was happening to me. They were circumstances that would make anyone ask the question, *what's the point?* I hadn't a single ounce of strength to do a thing about anything. I was still low. When you're low, you can expect that nothing is going to change until you do.

What I know is we're human, so take the time you need to be low. Get it all out. Every bit. Every drop. Then come back, reevaluate yourself, learn from your low, and move forward. Whatever you do, don't stay in the low. It's easy, but easy doesn't put change into motion.

At the time that's all I wanted to do. I stayed in my low for too long, simply watching my life roll along like a car without a driver. I was crashing into every wall on the way down, and I did nothing to stop it.

Even if you have no idea how to change the course of your life, start with what you do know. For me, all I wanted to do was to be happy again. Under all my sopping depression, hateful anger, livid resentment, clutching grudges, and crippling pain, that was all I truly wanted. I wanted to have my life driving toward a place I was excited to go, so that is where I started: with happiness.

Jim wanted me gone, but his parents said, "You can stay as long as you want." Their compassion never ceased to amaze me. So, I weighed my options.

1. *Crawl back to my father and the tumbleweed village.*

2. *Leave. Potentially be homeless.*

3. *Stay. Live with your ex-boyfriend. Hate every minute of it.*

Living with my family was entirely out of the equation. To me, there would never be a good enough reason in the universe to bring myself back to them. Truth be told, some of them didn't even want me back because of the arguments I had caused about the money issue. Being homeless didn't sound too terrible. I could sleep in my car, eat in the school cafeteria and shower in the locker room when necessary. Or the last, most undesirable choice: stay. I thought long and hard about this one. When I did, I started to wonder why I was leaving in the first place. *Because it would be awkward? Because I was embarrassed? Because since some guy decided we were no longer an item, I had to shuffle up the card deck of my life? Again! After just a month and a half? Really? Because of what he chose?* No.

Sure, Jim would eventually start seeing other girls. Sure, it would be mortifyingly awkward. Sure, I'd hate every second of it. But, I left my father's home because I'd had enough of other people making decisions for me. I had no clue how to make any of my own decisions, but I was damn well willing to try. I was determined to be happy again.

Oh, it was the least desirable choice, but I decided it was the result of his decision, not mine. So, in an effort to fight for my happiness, rule my own choices and allow other people to suffer the consequences of theirs, I chose to stay.

After all, I came back because I wanted to finish out the rest of my school year with my friends and graduate with my class. That's what was important to me. That was going to make me happy. I hadn't expected this curve ball to swing my life around, but I had no choice but to dance with it. Even if it meant living under the same roof with an ex-boyfriend who could no longer stand the sight of me.

I stayed.

And I was actually glad that I did.

...

May 2010

The last semester of my senior year was, without question, a most bizarre, inexplicable time. I made the badminton team and quit just days later. I talked to some cute new guys but disappeared after they said they liked me. I sternly decided I would not go to college, but days later I was determined to go. Trying to find happiness came with no ease. I learned that obtaining happiness can, ironically, be a very miserable task.

I retreated to my room and bailed on plans with friends, Mom still heavily on my mind. Emotions poured out at unexpected hours of the day like a volcano of erupting memories. I hadn't seen Caleb for months or Junior for weeks. I only kept in contact with them by phone. I missed our laughter together.

I saw no part of my life making sense. All the direction gods of the world could have been shouting **GO THIS WAY!** and I still would have missed my sign. Still, at the same time, I couldn't allow it to continue this way. I could no longer accept the depression that had already consumed so much of my life. I was motivated with every firing cell of my being to make something out of all this mess. This was going to bring me happiness.

But I couldn't see any signs. I thought I had none. I've since learned that signs will present themselves if and when we're ready and willing to pay attention. Oftentimes we're just too swaddled in our own emotional, chaotic nonsense to see them. So when you're looking for answers, bring your attention away from what is happening *inside* you and move it towards what is happening *around* you. Open your eyes wide! Opportunities will keep poking at you until you give them the time of day. Mine came in a couple different forms.

The first was when my friend Nikki asked me where I was going for college. When I sadly replied, "Nowhere," she urged me to reconsider and to immediately apply for the college she had been accepted to. I shrugged her off. She had parents to help her, so what could she possibly know about my struggle?

The second came during another leisurely weekend conversation with Jim's mother; she asked me the same thing. "Where are you going to college after you graduate?" I replied with the same, sad response, "Nowhere."

She looked at me, confused, "Why?"

I told her, "I can't afford it. I don't have the money."

At that age, I believed going to college was only for the wealthy. I believed if you had a rich family and a spectacular SAT score, you would have the opportunity and go into a field of your choice. I didn't have either. So instead, I was coming to accept the fate that I would continue to work my part-time job at the Oberweis Ice Cream Parlor.

She looked puzzled, "You know, there are government assistance programs that help people go to school, right?"

My ears perked up, "What?"

"Yeah," she continued, "Every year the government helps people attend school. Especially people in your situation."

"Really?"

"Yes!" She laughed at me, "You weren't gonna go to school because you thought you couldn't afford it?"

"Well, yeah." My mindset shifted, "I thought you couldn't go to college if you didn't have money."

"No!" she laughed.

With this revolutionary newfound information, I darted downstairs and started searching through websites upon websites of local colleges. I texted Nikki thousands of questions: what to do, what forms to complete, and how to do them. I could go to college! That night, I set up all my college accounts, completed all the government paperwork, and sent in applications to the schools I qualified for, I even included Nikki's school, and eagerly waited for their responses.

It was another choice I had made for myself.

. . .

Thankful doesn't even come close to describing just how overwhelmingly accomplished and fulfilled I felt on my high school graduation day. I'll forever be saddened by Mom's absence in times of celebration, but I was proud to have made it out of the stormy, muddy, hell-of-a-year that it had been. I imagine I would have been lying on the couch and receiving my diploma in the mail if I had stayed living out in the cornfield town. Or, I would have dropped out because of my grief and never received it at all. I know I wouldn't have made it without Jim and his family's kindness in having offered their home to me.

I was thankful.

That cup of thanks continued to spill over when, weeks later, I received my acceptance letter to Saint Xavier University where I would begin my undergraduate program for psychology. It bolstered the throttle of motivation I needed to fulfill a career I was passionate about and change my sticky mess-of-a-life. In my heart, I told Mom I would go all the way. I would climb the entire psychology ladder and get that PhD. So, without a question of a doubt, that is where my heart and mind set sail to for the next four years.

...

November 2010

After having been disappointed by my new school in 5th grade because it wasn't as fun as television made it up to be, I decided not to hold on to any expectations about college. However, after the school's formal welcome through freshman orientation, campus tours and floor meetings was all over, college quickly proved to be *exactly* how I'd imagined. Better, even. Welcome week hosted events like a courtyard movie night, outdoor foam party, battle of the sexes tug-o-war, water balloon fights and a number of creatively themed nights. All at once, I made dozens of new friends who I began meeting up with for lunch, football games and study sessions. But slowly, as the real work took hold and professors traveled farther into the syllabi, good grades started to become a serious ambition and the initial thrill leveled off. I kept my nose in my overly high-priced textbooks for the first few months and after a number of late study nights, I began looking forward to the relief of Thanksgiving break. As fate would have it, our family received an especially thankful holiday.

During my Monday night biology class at exactly 7:53 PM, as I was taking notes on my laptop, I was distracted by the relentless vibrations from my phone. I snuck it open as my professor lectured and read this text from my Tia Carlita:

They have just arrested that son of a b***** that murdered my sister. WOW! WOW! God is GOOD people!

I read it again. My eyes continued scanning the message again and again. Word by word. Carefully and slowly. Arrested? The word rang in my head.

I quickly and abruptly left class with all my belongings and retreated to the hallway to call her. I was calling forever with no luck until I saw her incoming call and quickly answered it. Her words brought it all to life, "They just arrested Ian!" she shouted.

"WHAT!!!"

"Yep, they just arrested him! They have him in custody now!"

I fell to my knees in the dark, empty hallway outside the auditorium of students, calmly learning about the molecular structure of who knows what. An epidemic of excitement, glorious gratification, and an indescribable rupture of joy came firing from deep within my soul. I took off, running to my dorm to share the blissful news with my best friend and roommate, Nikki.

Running across campus laughing with an incredibly large, hysterical smile and tears streaming down my face, I probably looked insane to all the casual students walking through the courtyards. I was overjoyed. I had to share the news with someone.

I arrived at the dorm to tell Nikki, but she was in the shower. Incapable of holding it in a second longer, I called Detective Bleecher, who I had met earlier that year. I was still catching my breath from the race across campus when he answered, "Hi, Detective Bleecher? I just received some news from my Aunt?"

"Well, your aunt is right!" he said joyously. "We arrested Ian outside the house tonight. He's at the station with us now and there will be a court date for his bond hearing soon. We..." he continued with more information, but my mind left the conversation to dance in the glory of *YES! He was finally arrested!*

Nikki came from the shower to see my drenched face, "Are you crying?" she asked. Simultaneously crying and laughing, I replied, "They just arrested Ian."

"Really!" She hugged me tight, and we were both in tears as we stood in our dorm room and rejoiced.

Confusingly enough, just weeks prior to this news, our family and friends had gathered at the court house with our team of attorneys and detectives asking them, "On a scale of one to ten, how much do we have right now to take this to court?" Our hopes were deflated with the response, "Right now, probably like a one or two."

Somehow, our hopes were being restored as Ian was walking into the station. He was being charged for first degree murder with a deadly weapon and concealment of a homicide. We all wanted to know what had happened in the past weeks that turned our sad stance from a pitiful one to a now joyous ten.

I didn't know how it had happened but I was simply grateful that he was now behind bars.

...

When the time finally came to regroup with our powerful female team of attorneys, they answered our question of *what changed?* And to our surprise, it was a lot.

Physical Evidence

- Tiny, almost microscopic bullet fragments, about 1/8 of a quarter's size, had been found on our garage floor hidden behind some dusty bins, cords and boxes; something Ian overlooked when he went back to clear up the scene. Fragments investigators believed belonged to the gun used.
- Small clumps of hair, presumed to be Mom's, were found on the cement floor.

Circumstantial Evidence

- Ian's timeline said he had just been at the bank and very possibly had just seen a large amount of money had been withdrawn from the account. The only other people who had access to the money were his sick mother and Mom. Grandma barely had the wits to know she had a son.

- Cell phone records showed Caleb and I attempted dozens of times to call Mom that Sunday. Ian tried twice.

- In our panic over Mom's disappearance, one of Caleb's phone calls to Ian's cell phone "pinged" off a nearby cell phone tower and was able to provide Ian's general location. It was only a few blocks away from where Mom and her car were found by police.

With all things considered, our team concluded there was enough physical evidence, circumstantial evidence, and historical evidence to make a case. *Hallelujah!*

Two quick days after the amazing news, I and other family members were gathered at the court house desperately waiting to discover what his bond would be. Neighbors, friends, family, pastors, distant relatives, everyone you could possibly imagine was there. Divided like a wedding, we all huddled on Mom's side, leaving empty spaces on Ian's side for people who never showed.

We arrived by 8:15 AM and sat patiently on the stiff, wooden benches. Wood covered the walls and a solid wooden banister separated the public seating from the lawyers, guards, judges and pending convicts.

We watched and listened to the cases before us. Other attorneys defended an accused man driving with a suspended license. Another man was accused of identity theft. Then there was a woman accused of child abuse.

Our whispered conversations went silent when a woman

called the familiar name, and a guard went to retrieve Ian from the locked, guarded door. My hand quickly latched onto Caleb's and squeezed it with tight anticipation.

Emerging in a black jumpsuit, Ian followed the guard up to the judge's podium. I could hear my heart pounding, and anxiety spread through me as the tiny hairs on my neck stood up. It was the first time I had seen Ian in eighteen months and in all that time he had made no attempts to ever reach out. Not to me and not to Caleb. Seeing him was like seeing a ghost.

They began. One of our attorneys stood at the judge's podium reading a long, detailed story about Ian's criminal history and the testimonies that Caleb and I gave of that Sunday. The judge sat before them, listening. After summing up the extensive, painful details of our past, Ian's attorneys rebutted by stating that he had a good job, had gone to college, and hadn't tried to flee. "We ask that you grant a reasonable bond," they pled.

Silence lingered and every ear listened intently as the judge sat there in contemplation.

After a long pause, he spoke, "Bail will be set in the amount of five million dollars." *Bang!* Oh, the blissful smiles that stretched across our faces as the guard immediately turned Ian around and walked him back through the secured door. Seated in the rows, our family exchanged looks of accomplishment.

I hadn't anticipated that it would become a chaotic day. No one else seemed prepared either. News reporters, camera crews and the former Illinois state attorney, Anita Alverez, were all present and were about to hold a small press conference outside the court room in the tall, tiled lobby.

The long, trailing line of us gathered behind the podium and camera lights as Mrs. Alverez spoke on the issue of domestic violence. We all stood together, Caleb by my side, and listened to her words. She had a few short minutes to sum up such a deep and complicated topic, one we all knew could have been filled with hours and hours more to say.

In front of the press, Caleb followed her speech and bravely spoke on our family's behalf. At fifteen years old, he had been forced into such a formidable role. I stood behind him, admiring the heck out of him and watched as all the faces focused on him.

After the press had their fill of questions, we all dispersed from the dreary, grey court house lobby. Our family headed outside to the chilly winter air, bundled in black coats and leaving through the spiraling exits only to be met with a reporter from ABC news, eager to have a personal word away from the chaos inside.

Again, Caleb was their target. I understood that his story was difficult and one the press wanted to expand on. I stood back as he was faced with a microphone. He remained strong and positive to the best of his abilities, trying to push a smile through the pauses.

Having Ian behind bars, even if only with pending uncertainty, made us feel safer. When he was still out, I worried that he'd find me at a gas station filling up my new car's tank and kidnap me. Although his arrest meant there was hope for Mom's justice and a chance for her peaceful rest, it also meant dealing with the whole atrocious mess in the form of important court dates, prepping for trial, receiving subpoenas, flying into town, retelling our story, flying out of town, changing court dates, taking off work, prepping for trial again, retelling our story again, listening to past and painful stories, discovering new painful stories, hearing new painful evidence, having nightmares about new evidence, having flashbacks to past stories, struggling with the trauma, trying to find peace, trying to move on, waiting for justice, waiting for peace and probably the worst, sickening and most dreadful part of it all: seeing his awful face after more than a year of not seeing Mom's.

This, my dear sweet friends, is the hideous, secret beast in the world of domestic violence.

Court.

. . .

Hating the Happy

THE VERY SIGHT OF THE GRAY, dreary Markham court house started to solicit dreaded anticipation. It was often that I didn't leave it the same as when I arrived. Over time, I simply lost count of how many times I walked in with hopes stretching to the skies only to leave with unsettling uncertainty and increased confusion. I was exhausted and held a fear of Ian's release. It seemed as if there was a constant follow up of when to come back and do it all over again.

There was no room for healing. One year turned into two, two into three, then three into four. It seemed to go on and on. Dates were rescheduled, cancelled, or delayed for countless reasons you couldn't even begin to imagine.

Our attorneys were ready. His, not so much.

They continually requested time; time, time, and more time. They were never quite up to speed on the case. For good lawyers, I understand the need to effectively represent your client, cross all your references, reexamine all the information, all the evidence, all the witnesses, prepare for any rebuttals and anticipate every argument. Yes, this I understand because our lawyers did that. However, his lawyers did not. If the definition of a good lawyer is to exhaust the prosecution enough to the point where everyone no longer has a sliver of hope for starting trial and has made the dream of justice seem like a distance mirage, then by this definition, he had outstanding lawyers!

Eventually, I became convinced the whole thing was a charade. I'd given up on the idea of going to trial. My once glimmering fight for justice turned into accepted failure.

I hoped Ian would throw in the towel and confess. It had been four years since Mom passed, three of which he had been held. Surely, he had to be tormented by his own demons. Surely, he would surrender.

Time continued to pass, and I continued doing all that I knew how, moving toward happiness and trying to completely forget my past.

...

December 2011

School is expensive. Especially when you're doing it all on your own without anyone's help while working a minimum wage campus job. I was a public safety officer checking student IDs as they entered the building. It was a job I was grateful for, because it allowed me to get all my homework done.

However, after one and a half years of being in college, I was faced with the harsh reality that I might have to drop out. It was my sophomore year, and I was short in paying for the spring semester. I panicked. How could I possibly gather up three thousand dollars in just a few short weeks before the deadline date?

There was no way. I figured I could always come back when I had the money, but I feared that meant college would be put on the back burner and would never happen. With the uncertainties life had been known to chuck my way, I didn't want to risk going off a path I was happy to be on.

I told my new boyfriend my predicament and his friend gave me an idea: write a letter. *Write a letter about what, the fact that I'm poor?* I thought. He explained to me that he had heard of people who had written very powerful letters to their school's chairman requesting financial assistance in order to remain in school. I had already learned life didn't care for whiners and complainers. I also knew I had made a promise, not only to Mom, but to myself as well.

So, I gave it a shot. I had nothing to lose. There were no better options and no bank account containing three thousand dollars.

With my future on the line, I took out my laptop and tried to write the most passionate, compelling, and dynamic letter possible. Many hours later, when it was to my liking, I personally walked across campus towards the finance department and handed my delicately crafted letter to a woman who told me, "Okay, we'll get back with you."

It was not the reaction I had been hoping for. I headed back to my dorm without an answer. I was dripping with motivation, but it pained me to know that holes in my wallet might mean putting my dreams on hold.

After the deadline for the final payment passed, I accepted nothing was to come of my letter. As the end of the semester grew near, I slowly began clearing out my room and packing up my things.   During the last week before break, my space was cleared and nothing but some clothes and toiletries remained. It was during that week I received a call from a woman in the finance department asking me to come in to meet with the Special Financial Aid officer. Confused, but ecstatic, I agreed.

The next morning, I raced over to the office. When I arrived, I knew something must have come from my letter, but what? I waited for a moment before I was called into a large office where I met with a kind looking, middle-aged woman. I felt almost as if I was being interviewed. She was dressed in professional attire and asked me a few questions about my letter: where did your motivation come from to pursue higher education; why do you want to continue here? When I explained to her where my drive came from, the meeting was quickly over. The whole sit-down talk lasted less than five minutes. Oddly, there was very little said.

I walked out of her office, still uncertain. I met back with the receptionist, who informed me, "You should be seeing the changes on your statement soon."

Baffled, I looked at her as if she was speaking another language. "Huh?" I managed to mumble.

"Your statement," she said slowly, "You'll be seeing the updated changes on your next statement."

"Oh," I said stunned. "Okay?"

"Have a good day."

I slowly walked out the main door scratching my head with my eyes crossed, "Thank you."

I scanned my balance every day for the last remaining days

of the semester and sure enough, to my surprise, my balance went from $0.00 to $3,000.00 and I came back with even more fuel in my make-it tank for the next semester. *Ahhh.*

...

May 2012

My luck from the last semester's Finance Gods would most certainly be my one and only warning to *keep it together, Monica.* I was certain money could become an issue again if I didn't pay close attention. And since I wasn't rolling in dough and wanted to keep pursuing my dream of college as well as avoid another money struggle, I decided to downsize.

Dad had divorced Lydia and moved to an apartment in another deserted corn field village. Only this village thrived off the college and nearly all of the town's residents had attended it. It was a small college town.

My disputes with my father had long been settled and when he moved, he offered his spare bedroom to me. I made the choice to cut out the cost of boarding, but I enjoyed my dorm experience and would have to leave all my friends. At the end of the spring semester, I moved out to the middle of nowhere in order to attend Northern Illinois University where I would start a lonelier, more affordable junior year. I needed to graduate, and things needed to change if that was going to happen.

...

August 2012

Aside from the swarm of intense classes, relentless professors and major, grade-dependent projects, I began noticing other unexplainable issues that year. Issues that began happening when I spent time with the people I loved the most.

No matter what the distance, Junior and I always kept a relationship. Our lives trailed off to different places because he moved around a lot, but we remained in each other's lives, and I tried to visit him in each new place he went.

At the start of my busy school year, he offered to take me out to lunch. He picked me up from campus, and we drove to a famous Chicago seafood restaurant he had seen featured on Top Chicago Restaurants. He was ready to splurge on the amazing crab legs and jumbo shrimp they were known for. We realized we had missed each other so much in the years of being apart, so we made it a regular effort to have lunch together whenever possible.

The second time we went out, he picked me up from the corn field land of Dekalb and drove off on the expressway towards Naperville. I couldn't tell you what on earth we were laughing about during the car ride, but it made my abs hurt in the best kind of way. It made me realize I hadn't laughed so hard in long time. Hysterically snorting in the passenger seat, I sat clenching my side and squeezing out happy tears. Glancing out the window as the world was passing by at eighty miles per hour, I was suddenly met with an awful thought; *What if we died, right now. What if we got into a terrible accident in this very, happy moment?*

As Junior continued laughing, my happy feelings instantly faded as I became immediately concerned with my terrible thoughts. I was laughing the hardest I'd laughed in months and couldn't understand what had just happened.

My laughter grew quiet and eventually stopped. Junior unknowingly continued adding to the happy nonsense we were giggling about, but in my mind, I was becoming deeply afraid. *Why had I thought up the worst possible thought at such a happy moment? I've never done that before.* I didn't understand. I brushed it off. *Stupid, you're just stupid,* I thought, and continued trying to enjoy our time together.

A few days later, the thought still consumed me, and I began waking up from the worst nightmares I'd ever had. Two or three nights out of the week, I'd wake up in a panic. I'd jolt out of my sleep from the sound of my own crying, my face and pillow sopping wet from tears. As the nightmares became more frequent, causing me to lose sleep, I started to pay closer attention to them. I realized I could barely remember the dreams that disturbed me. They would be present in my mind for the first few minutes I woke and then they would be gone. It was almost as if my mind gave me a glimpse of something, and then decided to delete it from my memory.

As the inexplicable thoughts and nightmares continued, so came another fear. I began to fear being behind the wheel of my own car. *What if I got into an accident and died, right now? Suddenly?* The thought alone would make me slow my speed. At school, there came more intrusive thoughts: *What if someone walked into this cafeteria and shot me right now?* The thought alone would make me leave my class. As each pressing thought rose, I would beat myself up. *What is wrong with you? Why are you doing this to yourself?* Red flags were firing, and I knew something wasn't right with me.

For weeks, the horrible, useless thoughts kept wreaking havoc in my day to day moments. It wasn't until the professor of my counseling class introduced the new assignment that I decided to reach out to someone. Our class was given two options. The first was to attend and write about your experiences through four counseling sessions. The second was to write about theories in counseling psychology. Since Mom was gone, I wanted to talk to someone and felt that with the wild, uncomfortable thoughts I was having, I needed to. I chose option one.

I set up my first appointment in the Student Center where I met with a woman near the end of her graduate program. She would be my counselor, and for an hour we sat in a private room with a one-way mirror. As I sat across from her making small talk, I avoided revealing the very subject I wanted to. I knew it would be for my benefit, that it was the very thing I was here for. Yet, being the counselor and being the counseled are two entirely different things.

I left the first session with just about nothing accomplished and was given a card with when to come back. My panicked nightmares and anti-happy thoughts continued, pushing me even more to wonder, *what the heck was wrong with me?* It felt as if my own mind wanted to self-destruct and was pressing the detonate button.

A week later in my next session, I decided to open up and tell her about one of the dreams I had the night before. She never pressured me to talk about anything I didn't want to. She was kind and patient, but I knew I wouldn't get anywhere if I didn't say what was on my mind. I had written out my dream as soon as I woke up that day, and I dug into my backpack, pulled it out and read it to her.

"January 16th 2014

Last night I had another completely horrible and terrifying dream. I know it was longer than what I remember, but all I can remember is this…

Mom was in my dream again and she gave me a gun. She said something like, 'it will make your pain go away'. This isn't exactly what she said and maybe she didn't say it at all. Maybe in the dream I just thought it to myself. But then after she handed me the gun, she left the room and then left the home. It was a home I had never been in before. I remember, I was crying as I held the gun and began shooting myself in the back of the head. I shot myself three times in the pattern of small pyramid; two shots at the bottom and one on the top middle. I wasn't dying. I didn't die in my dream, but I remember my head was aching and pounding. I started to bleed and began to panic. I looked in a drawer nearby and pulled out a pink bandana, one I actually have in my nightstand. I tied it around my head to apply pressure on where I had shot myself. Then I left the house crying, frantic and looking for help. I wanted someone to take me to the hospital.

In my dream, I didn't understand why I didn't die from the shots, which made me even more frantic and scared. I remember when I walked outside the house, people came rushing to me. They were people I knew in the dream but can't recall from real life. They looked at the back of my head, touched the blood and I remember seeing the blood on both our hands. I told them, "I need to go to a hospital" and that's when I woke up.

When I woke up, my head hurt and starts to even now when I think about this dream."

With my therapist sitting across from me, I sat with my head down grabbing tissue after tissue to catch my rapidly falling tears. I couldn't imagine how disturbed I appeared to her. She sat silently as she indulged me in the moment of pain that had come over me as I released everything. I didn't understand why I was having the thoughts or the nightmares I was, but when the last word left my mouth, it was in that exact instant I realized what was wrong with me. They weren't just nightmares. They weren't just horrible thoughts, and they weren't happening simply to torment me. It was trauma.

Everything I had been trying to break free from had caught up with me four years later. In any way possible, my body was trying to warn me that underneath all my motivation, all my drive, and all my resilience, I wasn't okay. I hadn't dealt with anything yet. I was only avoiding it and trying to leave it behind.

To my reader, I feel it is important to say that at this time I was in no way suicidal. There's a big difference between having suicidal thoughts with and without intention. I had no intention to pursue suicide. Instead, I was traumatized. I was suffering from symptoms of post-traumatic stress disorder, because I was actually afraid of death.

I feared loss. I feared losing anyone at all, especially in the way I had lost Mom. I was deeply afraid that anyone I loved or would ever love again would leave me. I worried at every given minute. After hanging up the phone I couldn't help but think the worst: *Would that be the last time I was going to speak to that person?* Joyously driving in a car while laughing hysterically would quickly become a terrible memory of: *Is this the last moment I will have with this person?* When walking to class: *Could I suddenly be shot by some maniac and never have the opportunity to fulfill any of my biggest, boldest dreams? In the same way Mom was never able to fulfill hers?*

I knew my thoughts were irrational, but that didn't stop me from believing them, feeling them, fueling them, and manifesting them.

Long after the assignment was submitted and graded, I continued going to therapy every week for the next four months. During that time, I made lists of all the things I would miss about Mom. I would write down all the things I would never get to do with her, experiences I would never have, memories I never wanted to let go of, and thoughts I needed to get rid of.

My fear seemed to grow out of control the more I exploited it. It came to the point where I was terribly afraid of simply having a good time. I couldn't enjoy anything because, to me, that would have meant something bad was about to happen. With no understanding of how to fix my own thoughts, I buried my nose in my books, hoping it would fix itself or just go away.

This was not how I wanted to live. My mind was becoming my biggest problem, trapping me inside my own thoughts. I felt like there was no way to get out of it.

Therapy, I've learned through personal and professional experience, helps us to see the things we don't even know exist. We think we're stuck. We think there's no way out, but our thinking is most likely already flawed. So in these moments, we're not being rational and we can't trust ourselves or our thoughts. We need to seek professional help.

I still continue to seek therapy whenever I need help finding answers. In every therapy journey I've taken, I realize that all the answers I ever needed were within me. I had them all along, but just needed help in pulling them out.

After sixteen meetings, my last session ended with a peaceful, new perspective. I had taken small, infant steps to rearrange my thought process and heal from losing Mom. In no way was I "healed" in the way most people think therapy works, but I did have something. I saw I had a chance to heal. It was something I don't think I had before. I certainly didn't have the tools like I did now.

Painfully, I had to accept that my relationship would never again be the same with Mom. I had lost her, and I feared death because of it. I told myself this didn't mean I had to stop having a relationship with her altogether. It didn't mean I had to say goodbye and move on in my life without her. There would never again be that precious face to face relationship, but I could still have a spiritual relationship. I could still talk to her whenever I wanted. I could still look to the heavens for her guidance. I could still believe that she would be my guardian angel and the cheerleader of my life. She would always be with me, no matter what. Your thoughts and your beliefs are your choice. This is what I chose to believe.

...

Desolate Places

April 2014

CALEB HAD EMBARKED ON HIS JOURNEY into college with the
diehard motivation of becoming an actor. One day he's going
to be great! He had graduated from high school as valedictorian and presented an enticing speech to a stadium filled with
parents, staff, graduates, and supporting family, one of whom
was a crazy sister screaming with wild excitement far up in the
bleachers. Me.

Junior was using every ounce of motivation within him
to stick to one career and was moving up his professional ladder. He also became a father to a beautiful baby girl, born in
November of 2013. She was given Mom's middle name as her
own, Rosa. Just a couple of short months later, Junior's wife was
again pregnant, and eventually gave birth to a sweet baby boy.
He was given Dad's name as his middle name, Martin. To this
day, when I look at their soft, smiling faces I'm reminded of the
grandmother Mom never thought she would become. When
I'm around them, being pulled in every direction, I imagine

Mom would have easily had her hands full, and I picture their faces smothered in red lipstick kisses.

At the same time, I was gearing up for the end of my last semester of college. The senioritis was real. I had final projects, exams and papers to complete along with graduation plans and fees quickly approaching. All our lives were driving as far away from our past as possible, but court still lingered in the shadows. Mom's memory hadn't rested, and Ian was still technically innocent in the eyes of the law.

I communicated back and forth with our attorneys every couple of months via email, phone and text. I would get word that trial was set and arranged for one day, which left me tossing and turning in the approaching nights. But then I would receive an update that the trial was postponed…again. The constant jerk of emotions left me exhausted. The disappointment was eating away all my hope. *It'll happen when it happens* was the mentality I had developed.

For five years, my emotions had been playfully toyed with by Ian's lawyers. There was no sign of a guilty plea or even an insanity plea. He had changed lawyers for the third time and each time he did, another several months would pass, allowing the new lawyers time to get up to speed. At one point, one of our attorneys told me, "I've never been involved with a case that dragged on this long. This is unheard of."

Maybe it was a tactic, I thought, *Push the judge to the edge.* Perhaps they were banking on the judge becoming so frustrated after their million, ridiculous requests for more time that he might finally deny them. Because if he had, Ian's lawyers could throw the whole trial right in the trash whenever they wanted by referring back to the time the judge didn't allow them the additional time they had asked for to prepare. They could potentially ask for an entirely new trial: a retrial.

At this stage, I learned more than I cared to about the legal system. The first lesson was, it's strict. The second lesson was that it can consume what feels like the rest of your life simply by waiting for a trial to begin.

...

May 2014

The semester was over. I submitted my final projects, completed all my final exams, and turned in my graduation dues. The victorious day came. It was finally time to walk across the stage.

On graduation day, I woke just barely before the sun and started to hear the rest of my family slowly rising as I began getting ready. It was a day I had dedicated to Mom a long time ago.

As I leaned over my dresser, inching closer to the mirror to apply my eye makeup, I was reminded of Mom and how she stood in the bathroom getting ready every night. Just as everything reminded me of Mom on other days, today I could feel her everywhere.

I styled my hair and finished my makeup, striving for perfection. My cleanly pressed cap and gown smiled at me as it hung over the closet door. I smiled back with sheer bliss and imagined Mom was over my shoulder.

Hung on my bedside portrait of Mom, I kept my most precious items. There was a shining, elegant gold ring inlaid with five shining diamonds and a graceful silver chain-link bracelet decorated with a solid heart charm. These were the only pieces of Mom's jewelry I had. They were the pieces of her that I made sure were coming with me on this day.

My bright dress and vibrant jewelry matched my feelings of that day. An hour later, with my nails done, heels on, and hair carefully swept to my side, I was ready.

I opened the door and was welcomed with congratulations by Dad and Caleb. We enjoyed a short breakfast together, but my nerves were barely letting me eat. I wanted to leave and arrive early for the pre-graduation assembly.

When I arrived at the convention center, the happy reality of the day set in at the sight of caps, gowns, tassels and robes filling the room. I found my place in line according to the "M" of my name and gently placed on my cap and gown, taking in the exciting energy of the atmosphere. The nervous chatter was loud and eager smiles appeared on everyone's face.

After chatting with my own friends and taking pre-graduation photos, the staff coordinators called for our attention. Everyone dispersed and took their places back in line. The sudden silence screamed in anticipation.

Walking out to the stadium filled with people, with flashing camera lights and blinding spotlights, I searched for my family. I found Caleb waving hysterically for my attention in the same passionate way I had at his graduation. Glancing at the people beside him, I saw the rest of my family shouting and waving too. Once I knew it was them, I flailed my arms in the air to let them know, *Yes, I see you there!* I had a smile so wide and strong that my face hurt after the entire ceremony.

Professors, valedictorian, and other educated nobles presented riveting speeches. They praised all the graduates for having made it there and for their accomplishments. I was still trying to believe I was sitting in this seat. I visualized a snapshot of every obstacle, obstruction, interference, struggle and loss I had overcome to make it here to this seat, to this stadium, with this cap, this gown and this tassel.

Four years ago, I didn't even believe I was capable of going to college. Now, I was sitting with a sea of college graduates ready to embark on a new life and be handed a diploma. Having hurdled over exams, quizzes, projects, presentations, finals, readings, late study nights, solo study nights, group study nights and questioning myself every step of the way, I was *more* than prepared to get my hands on that kickass piece of paper. In spite of the hurt and pain I had been sorting through, there was no questioning myself anymore.

My name was called. I walked across the stage, flipped my tassel, shook some professor's hand and latched onto that diploma. While hundreds of people watched, I couldn't help but do a little dance as I walked down the aisle back to my seat. *Finally! I did it!* All of my efforts were for Mom.

During the many congratulations, swarm of photos, celebratory dinner, toasts and speeches gathered with my brothers, father, boyfriend and his parents, I was still thinking about the one person I had to celebrate this day with. Immediately after dinner, Junior, Caleb and I drove the hour up to the peaceful cemetery to celebrate with Mom. In my heart, this day was hers more than it was mine.

...

Adapted

December 2016

LIFE IN THE FIELD OF MENTAL HEALTH, I learned, was immensely harder than any of my professors had indicated. In fact, I don't feel any of them prepared me for the emotional stress and uncomfortable decisions I would be expected to make for grown adults who had no shame, or for elderly people who had no support and were wandering the streets homeless. They did not prepare me for the wild, savage children who were swearing by the age of four or the alcoholics who spat on me when I told them no more beds were available in the hospital. It's a rugged road with many potholes. The only glimpse I was ever given came from a professor who told the class at the beginning of the semester, "Do not go into this field to make money. If that is your motivation, you are in the wrong field." He was absolutely correct about that, but he never explained why.

I hadn't understood how learning about psychology would transfer into practicing psychology. Although my educators skipped over informing me on how my bachelor's degree could be applied in the real world, I ended up finding a job as a case manager at a mental health hospital. Turns out, I was really good at it.

Moving to Florida with my boyfriend after graduation was exactly what I needed. The sunshine state provided me with the start I needed to set off on a new life and box up my old past and leave it in the attic. After dating for three years, we moved into a cozy one-bedroom apartment under the sun with the sea and palm trees around us. After two years of adjusting to my new sea shell searching and kayaking lifestyle, I received an inevitable tug at my heartstrings.

There was another notice that the trial was starting in December. They assured me it was really happening. But I decided I wasn't going to believe it until I was up there on that stand. I couldn't handle the emotional tug-o-war any longer, and I was in a happy place with where my life was going.

Our team of attorneys was as fried and dried with this case as we were. In my heart and head, I had moved on a long time ago. I had set off into a new life, but Ian was still a piece of my past that was drawing me back. Praying that he would confess was hopeless. I knew that he would never submit his control or admit defeat, but when would this end? So many years had passed that I questioned how many more would have to continue to go by before this was all laid to rest. *How much longer would he try to keep us in his grasp?*

My doubt was still there after my flight was booked, and we were scheduled to depart on a Saturday in just a few short weeks. The trial was scheduled to begin on Monday. *Okay, not a big deal. There's still loads of time for this thing to fail,* I thought. When those weeks passed, and I was standing in the airport security line, I started to rethink this. It was the first time I had come as far as flying out for trial. I suddenly realized that maybe this was going to happen after all.

On the two-and-a-half-hour flight to Chicago, my mind raced with the vivid thoughts of our family's day in court. A disturbing possibility came over me that I had tried to ignore for so long; *What if he's not found guilty?* That thought alone made me sick, but I had to consider the rotten reality. *What if he is found innocent and walks? He will have gotten away with committing a cold, unforgiving murder. No punishment, ever. And no justice, ever, for the years of hurt he brought upon Mom. The system has been known to fail people before, so why would I be any different? Why would Mom be any different to them?* My heart ached as I thought about the possibility. There was a chance our family might never have peace, and I feared it. Imagining any other reality than one with a guilty verdict was unbearable. It was easy for my thoughts to run wild and drag me along for the ride, but I had to shut them off if I was going to get through these next crucial days.

When I arrived in Chicago at the O'Hare Airport, I waited for Junior outside the terminals as the freezing air swiped my cheeks. He pulled up in his pristine, white taxi car, tossed my belongings into his trunk and slammed it shut. "How's it going siiiiis!" He smiled.

"Whassup my brotha!" I answered. He hugged me with so much strength my feet came off the ground. The busy airport allowed no time to linger, so I quickly opened up the car door, hopped in the passenger seat and welcomed the warm air on my face and fingers. As he sped off, I looked upon him with admiration. I hadn't seen him in months since moving to Florida and he too, had changed so much since Mom passed away. Fatherhood had forced him to make a plan for his life and for the kids. I was proud to see that he had been working with the same taxi company for seven years and putting in over 40 hours each week. He had a goal to become the owner or at least manage enough drivers, so he could spend more time being a father. It wasn't like Junior to be so motivated, but I know that losing Mom created the same fire in him that it had in me. He was doing the best he had ever done with his life. It was the kind of best that Mom was always trying to get him to fight for, and I was proud of him for having achieved it.

After catching up on what's new with one another, we began talking about the trial. Both of us were nervous and uncertain. We tried to provide one another with encouragement and avoided thinking like I had been on the flight.

The next morning, my nerves were at a consistent high as I prepared myself for court the following day. We set out to go see Dad in DeKalb amidst the cornfields and grey winter skies. As we were driving on a vacant highway, all my stress became pointless. As fate would have it, I received a phone call from our lead attorney, Jennifer, that Sunday. She had the inevitable news: even though court was scheduled to begin in less than twenty-four hours, she told me it had been postponed.

"I'm so sorry," Jennifer said. "The defense filed a motion that..."

I drifted away from her words and was stuck on the fact that we would have to wait again for who knows how long. Jennifer was a very tall, slender woman with shoulder length black hair and thick, black glasses over her large, kind eyes. Her voice was bold yet calm, and she almost always wore a suit when

I saw her. She had been on our case since the beginning and by her constant reassurance I knew she was doing everything in her power to make sure Mom had justice. But there was still so much that was beyond her control. My patience and mental strength were entirely deflated, and I was angry at myself for being so foolish in thinking this was almost over.

Having been disappointed more times than I can recall and being involved with one of the longest cases our attorneys had ever been a part of, I strongly suspected that because of the deranged world Ian lived in, this was somehow intentional; that this was all possibly his doing; that in the past eight years he forced us to stay right there with him. Having us in court every couple of months meant he still had some control in our lives. It began to feel like torture, and I sensed he was involved. I had no choice but to continue hitchhiking down what felt like a hopeless road, praying somewhere, someday, there would be an end to his reign in our lives.

...

March 2017

Months after our last disappointment, I received another no-tification from Jennifer. The trial would be starting in August. *Pshhhhhhh*, I instantly thought. *Yeah, okay! You got it!* I thought nothing of it. Defeat had owned me, and I felt as if Mom had been let down.

I came to believe that Ian would continue to toy with us until he died out of pure manipulative control. I knew that he was in awful shape, so I saw it as a valid plan for him. Jail and age had not been kind to him. He had lost over fifty pounds and weighed less than I did. He even seemed to grow shorter. The skin was slipping right off his cheeks. He looked brittle, thin and pale, having almost no muscle left on his body. I remembered how he had shown off his large biceps to Mom during one of our visits to him in prison and how sick it made me to think Mom was attracted to him. Now, there was almost nothing left of him. All of him was leaving as his body drifted off into the wind. He was ill. He had been diagnosed with a thyroid disease and other health issues. But our family was so calloused towards Ian and his manipulative ways that we even suspected his sickness could have been intentional. We believed it was a possible lure to sway the jury into believing he was a sad, frail, elderly gentleman struggling with his health. My jaded heart had little sympathy for him, and after years of being witness to his award-winning performances, I was unable to believe a single thing he did or said. I looked back on his entire life as a mere act. He always had a plot with deeper intentions.

Nevertheless, our attorneys assured us that the trial was going to begin on Monday, August 7th. But I refused to believe it was going to happen until I was standing on that podium giving my testimony. The months passed and the date came closer, but still, I thought nothing of it. I continued to work, relax and go out with friends as normal. Court was never coming. End of story.

I denied it, continued going forward, and soon there was only a week left until trial was set to begin. All my travel arrangements were made, and my flight ticket was sitting in my email, just waiting to be printed. Jennifer called me days before I was scheduled to fly out just to check in and assure me that no bumps seemed to be in the road. Court was a go.

Since I had strongly convinced myself that trial would always continue to dangle in the future, instead of the here and now, I never even imagined what the day would be like when it actually came. When it did, I felt entirely unprepared and out of sorts. Even so, I don't believe anything could have prepped me for what I was about to endure.

...

August 7, 2017

At Junior's Chicago home, I awakened to the sun blazing through the kitchen window. My air mattress had started to deflate and was shouting at me to get up anyway. My niece and nephew came in, showering me with hugs and kisses as they dressed for daycare at an upsetting 5:30 AM. I squeezed and kissed them before they went off and tried to grasp the fact that today had started. Junior, Caleb and I were scheduled to be at the court house by 8:00 AM.

As if awaking in a dream, the morning felt surreal. I was ready and dressed much earlier than I needed to be. I didn't apply any makeup, because I knew my tears would smear anything I put on.

Caleb continued sleeping on the couch. He woke up minutes later, and both he and Junior began getting dressed in black pants and dress shirts. The mournful sense of the day felt similar to the morning we had dressed for Mom's funeral, and I couldn't help but take myself right back to the awful feelings of those days. I remembered how I sat in the dark limo with the bright orange funeral sticker when my family and I went to the burial service. I was stiff, fearing what awaited us. As I sat in Junior's kitchen, I felt the same fear. I looked down at my heels and could hear my thoughts whispering, *You have to accept she's gone.*

Her silver charm bracelet and gold ring were the only jewelry on my right hand and I needed them now more than ever. Each of us kept quiet and were deep in thought as the time to leave drew nearer. There had been no indication that court would be cancelled, but with 2 hours still ahead, I didn't doubt that it could be.

We finally settled into Junior's car and took off to the court house. The day was gloomy, and the sun I had become so familiar with in Florida was hidden behind a blanket of grey clouds. The light laughter between us during the forty-minute drive dispersed when we arrived at the dreary, dark brown building with cathedral glass windows and long, wide concrete steps leading to the entrance. It was a place I never wanted to become so familiar with.

As we were being shuffled through security for the hundredth time, we were spotted by a familiar face. "You're Carlita's nephew, aren't you?" The female guard noticed Caleb, who was always easily identified by his bold, wavy locks which I convinced him to slick back into a neat bun after the long argument we had earlier that morning about looking presentable. She waved us off with "Good luck, guys!" and we all quickly sped to the second floor to meet with our attorneys.

When we arrived in the library waiting room, we were greeted with many familiar faces sitting at the tables. My dad, tias, family friends, cousins, Mom's divorce lawyer, the detectives from the case, Mom's coworkers; and all who would be testifying.

"Hey guys, how are you doing? You ready?" Jennifer asked, always keeping a positive attitude.

"Yeah, we're okay. Nervous." I shrugged.

"Don't be nervous, you guys are more than prepared."

I smiled, trying to believe her.

"Okay, so Monica will be going first, and then…" What my ears heard nearly made my knees collapse. I knew that I would be testifying soon, I just didn't think soon equaled first. I had told the same story millions of times and reiterated the same horrific details a million and one more. I had recapped all the key points of that awful Sunday and been prepped by the attorneys more times than I could count. It was so familiar that I started to feel confused, and I shook in terror as I imagined answering incorrectly to a question I'd long known the answer to.

"The defense wants to file a couple of motions, but we're confident they'll be thrown out." Her confidence allowed the reality to sink in: today was the day she had prepared us for.

"Okay, so we'll see you guys downstairs!" she said as she smiled and left pushing a large cart with boxes of evidence and paperwork down the hall while the other two female attorneys followed her.

As the rest of us sat waiting together in the library with the trial merely minutes away, I panicked. *Oh my God, you're going first. I hate going first with anything! Ugh, I've never been that kind of person. I don't have that kind of confidence. I can't do it.* Trying to get the thought out of my head, I attempted to chime in with family conversations around me. But the strain and tension of my thoughts made it impossible to concentrate on anything else.

Detective Bleecher arrived in uniform with his blonde hair nicely combed and a large, comforting smile that could make anyone feel safe. We all had many questions and he politely answered them as best he could.

"What's going to happen if he's found guilty? Or innocent? What's going to happen this week? Today? When do you testify? How long will this take?" We all continued, "Is there a chance he could walk?" Detective Bleecher was head of the investigation team that started on our case years ago and even he, himself, was scheduled to testify.

I wasn't informed until the very last minute that because of how sensitive our case was; no one was allowed to sit in the courtroom while others were giving their testimony. There was too much at stake with this case, and the judge wanted no reason for a mistrial. That meant I couldn't even have Caleb in the court room when I took the stand. Instead, Caleb waited upstairs with the other people who would be testifying while everyone else filled the seats of the court room.

During our conversation with Detective Bleecher, a woman appeared at the doorway grabbing everyone's attention.

"Monica, they're ready for you." Her words forced everyone's eyes upon me.

I jolted out of my seat and felt a rush of intense hesitation. Everyone quietly whispered 'good luck' and 'you got this' as I walked with stone feet out the door with the woman. I followed her downstairs, and she led me to a small waiting area and break room that was right behind our assigned court room. I sat next to a man wearing a black button up and jeans who had reported to police eight years ago that he had seen a tall Hispanic male leave the driver's side of a clean, white Pontiac late that

Sunday afternoon. In his testimony, he said that the tall Hispanic man walked around to the trunk of the car, opened it and gently brushed something inside of it. The man watched from the window of his living room as the unknown Hispanic man across the street stared inside the trunk of the Pontiac for what felt like a moment too long.

After that, the man reported that the Hispanic male closed the trunk, wiped it down, returned to the driver's seat, and took off. His testimony greatly improved our case because his description of the Hispanic male was nearly in perfect harmony with Ian's appearance. I believe Ian was staring at Mom as she lay motionless in the trunk.

As I waited with the man in jeans, he began to talk of how awful this all was, "How could someone do something like this?" At the table was a female guard ordering lunch for dozens of people and becoming frustrated with the service on the other end of the line. With a simple smile I quietly nodded in agreement to the man's comment. My legs were shaking so hard I was more focused on trying to stop them.

"I just told them what I saw. A man went to the trunk and looked like he was looking at something inside. Then he took off." Already on the edge of my nerves, my volcano of tears nearly erupted when he asked, "How did you know her?" I took a deep breath.

"I'm her daughter," I replied. When I looked up, I saw his eyes widen as he leaned back in his chair.

"I'm so sorry," he said, and his face grew more serious. *Hmm, those words again,* I thought. I was never quite sure how to feel about them.

A moment later, a bailiff opened the door to the court

room and called my name, "Monica?"

I rushed up and walked behind the guard as he led me into the court room. When I came to the front, I felt like I had never had so many faces staring so intently at me. I took a step up to my seat on the stand which was positioned right next to the judge. He was an Italian man with a wide face and thick features. His tiny glasses were kept at the end of his large nose and he wore a noble, black robe.

Our attorneys had made every effort to keep him as our judge since the beginning of this case. He was a fair judge, they said. And after all these years, in some weird way, I felt like I knew him, even though we had never spoken a word until now.

Trembling had now spread to my entire body and reached an all-time high. My seat in the stand was high enough to overlook almost everyone in the court room. I could see the familiar faces of Mom's amazing team of loved ones directly ahead of me, all sitting behind the dark wooden divider. Dad and Junior were there in the first row.

I hadn't expected the row of jurors would be so close to my right-hand side. The twelve members were sitting a mere three feet away, but it felt as if they were sitting on top of me. I could feel their eyes studying me. I glanced at each of them, trying to guess who might vote in our favor.

I tried to avoid his scolding and piercing stare, but there in front of me was Ian, finally sinking his teeth into me. He sat at a long conference table in the middle of the court room between the prosecuting and defense attorneys. Large glasses hung at the end of his thin nose, and he was dressed in a professional red shirt and tie that seemed two sizes too large for him. He had aged so much since I last seen him he was almost unrecognizable.

I stood up, raised my hand and was sworn in. I sat back down, and the judge reminded me to speak loudly for everyone to hear. It was something that always went against my natural instinct to speak softly. And then it began.

Jennifer took the podium, "Please state your name for the jury."

"Monica Mercedez Medina." I could hear the trembling in my voice which instantly infuriated me. *Stop it, don't be afraid. Speak with confidence. You can do this.*

Jennifer began by asking me the same questions she had asked me time and time again after years of repeated preparation, "What do you do for a living? How old are you? Can you identify him in court today? Describe what he's wearing."

As I sat there with all eyes and ears fixed upon me, I was still waiting for someone to tell me court had been cancelled.

Jennifer then began to ask the difficult questions, "Can you tell the jury what happened that day? Can you describe what you saw?"

"You have to speak up!" The judge interrupted my response and deflated the little confidence I was trying to build.

My shaking nerves may have been plain to see, but no matter how afraid I was, I pulled out every effort deep within me not to show it. I told the same story I had many times before, "When I got home I went downstairs to do my homework."

"What happened next?" she continued.

"I heard a knock at the door and I saw it was Caleb. He was holding Mom's purse in his hand and asked me why it was there. I told him I didn't know, and he said it had been on the floor. Then he pointed to her shoes in the back of the garage."

"Could you show us on the screen where he found them?" she replied. In front of the room was a large screen displaying the photos of our garage for the jury and all to see.

After walking over to the screen and indicating the location, I returned to my seat and continued with an easy breath, "Caleb showed me his things on the basement floor and said he had put them in Mom's trunk just a couple of days ago."

"What did you do next?"

"I called Mom and when she didn't answer, I called Ian."

"Did either of them answer?" she asked.

"No," I replied looking over at Ian.

Jennifer continued to lead me through the events of that day, "When you saw Ian at the door, what did you do?"

"Caleb asked him where Mom was," I replied.

"And what did Ian say?"

"He said he didn't know. That he was out for a walk."

"And how did he appear to you?"

"He was sweating. He seemed nervous. Anxious. Not like himself at all."

"Had you ever known him to take walks before?" she asked curiously.

"No."

With that, Jennifer came to a closing, "No further questions, your Honor."

She took her seat at the end of the conference table smiling at me with an expression that said *you did good*. Just two seats down from her was Ian. I avoided his glare and tried to focus on his attorney who stood up and prepared himself at the podium ahead of me.

He was a bald, black male with small, frameless glasses and

a large, square-shaped head sitting atop his perfectly trimmed grey suit. He had a mustache speckled with gray hair that he brushed as he readied himself. Behind the podium, he looked me up and down over his glasses as if preparing to make the best fool of me that he could. I had not the slightest idea what his questions were going to be.

The solid bench I sat behind was so tall that no one could see below my chest. My trembling hands were tugging so hard at each other that I'm convinced I could have pulled off my own finger and not noticed it.

The man began with the type of attitude that said *let's see if she knows what she's talking about.* He walked towards me with a sway in his step and began firing away. With each question, he slowly revved up a fury within me that I didn't even know I had. He questioned my relationship with Ian and attempted to force me into the role of an evil stepdaughter. He insinuated that *I never really liked Ian anyway, so this must be the only reason I was pointing the finger.*

He emphasized that since I was Caleb's older sister, I must have brainwashed Caleb into thinking horrible things about his own father. The man harshly added that I was too young when the first shooting occurred between Ian and Mom on Mozart, so I could have easily misconstrued what happened that night, and that for all I knew, Mom could have been the person to open fire all those years ago.

"You don't know, do you? You didn't see what happened, did you?" He walked up and down, implying that Mom could have easily been the instigator.

"They were arguing and…"

"So, they were arguing with each other, correct? She was

arguing with him and he was arguing with her, correct?" The influx of his voice made me angrier.

Mom, with her caring eyes and loving heart was the problem in all of this! Mom, with her small, short stature was the instigating factor in their entire relationship! Mom, with her soft flowing curls and vanilla scented perfumes, was the uncontrollable abuser! Poor Ian, was no more than a victim of Mom's uncontrollable rage?

They were the most absurd and offensive descriptions anyone had ever offered me about my Mom. The lawyer was attempting to disgrace and demean Mom's entire life of abuse, fear and hostility by blaming her as being an aggressive, violent woman. It was ridiculous! This lawyer's arrogant nonsense was starting a fire inside of me.

He was a complete stranger analyzing and questioning the most fearful and traumatic parts of my past and throwing my emotional distress out the window, just as if I had made it all up. He fired his bullet-like questions at me one right after the other and left me no time to form a thought or precise response. He pushed me, enraged me and desperately tried to destroy me. No one had ever examined me with such outrageously disturbing questions before, and no one had ever tried to manipulate me into pointing the finger at Mom and completely ignoring the evil in Ian.

I nearly exploded. I squeezed Mom's bracelet that circled my wrist until my hands turned blue. I tried to conjure up her presence, a guardian angel, or the Lord Jesus Christ; anything to help me regain the composure and focus I felt I was losing.

While I sat there behind the wooden bench, I saw Ian's eyes focused on me for the longest time as if he was waiting for me to crack. He appeared to be studying me spitefully and with deep resentment, as if my testimony had somehow betrayed him.

He was facing the rest of his life in prison, so I knew he wanted to grab a hold of anything to save himself. I knew his glare was no more than another attempt to strike fear within me. He wanted to distract me and regain any amount of control that he could.

Suddenly, I reminded myself I was a different person. I was no longer the same timid child he knew he could so easily torment. I was no longer the same adolescent who had been afraid to speak up. I was now an adult, ready to regain the voice he had stripped from me during all those years. I was in the court to speak the truth for every listening ear, the same truth that Mom was never able to tell. *Get a hold of yourself, you can do this. You've been waiting your entire life for this. Stop looking at him. Don't let him rush you, take your time. Don't answer a confusing question, ask him to repeat it. You're not the fool. You're strong. You're smart. You're doing this for Mom. Speak for Mom! You know the truth, speak it! Dear Lord, please help me to speak the right words.*

In the sea of staring faces, I could only think of Mom's face and how badly I did not want to let her down. I caught my breath, clenched my hands and released all of the rising tension inside of me. I fueled my anger into bold confidence.

I paused when necessary and responded firmly. I listened to his questions intently, my focus at a level it had never been at before. Every molecule of energy I had was centered on his words.

Finally, he released me. "No further questions, your Honor." I sighed in deep relief, shaking with a different kind of fear now. I was exhausted and felt like I had been running for miles. My part was done. There was nothing more I could do.

Badgering the Witness

MY MIND SPIRALED INTO A PLACE of both horror and peace as reality settled in, and what had been a long-dreaded moment finally passed. The most I could have ever done for Mom was behind me. After my part was over, I sighed with relief, but dreaded what still remained to be done.

Everything left was entirely out of my control. I weighed my entire past, present and future upon the outcome of this trial. The judge, jury and attorneys were all there just to try a murder case. But for me and my loving brothers, we sought so much more.

We would be restored when Ian was punished. Every piece of ourselves that Ian ever took away, every moment he scared us into silence, every hand he ever laid on us, every tactic he attempted, every lie he ever told, every tear Mom cried and every sleepless night he kept us in fear would no longer be ignored and unanswered.

I considered all the options until I could no longer think

straight and felt exhausted from all my tears. Aside from the importance of the verdict in our own lives, how could Mom's spirit ever rest if Ian was not convicted for the lifelong torture he had put her through?

The pressure was crippling. I had jumped in the shark tank hoping and praying I didn't get bitten, attacked or end up losing a limb. I just kept wading in the water and grew exhausted as I watched the large fins swim past me and prayed that I could just keep breathing. With each passing moment I was surprised I hadn't been torn to pieces, but I was ready, waiting for the first bite to strike. Sitting on those wooden benches, I was merely keeping afloat while the sharks of fate circled. I walked with numb legs back to the waiting area where Caleb waited for his turn on the stand.

"How was it?" he asked, his eyes seeping with curiosity.

"I don't know. I think it went okay." I was upset with myself. In the midst of Ian's lawyers questioning me, I felt like I could have responded better.

As strangers gave their testimonies, my family and I tried to pass time by grabbing drinks of water, coffee, and snacks from the friendly staff. Soft laughter, nervous smiles were accompanied by moments of light conversation that attempted to break the heavy tension of the room.

Moments later, the same woman entered in the doorway loaded with those anxiety-riddled words, "Caleb, they're ready for you."

His eyes widened, and his hands brushed against the armrests as he prepared himself. I could do nothing but offer him encouragement, "You got this."

Caleb was never good with his words. Even to this day,

we often laugh about how he might use one hundred words to describe what I could explain in ten. Out of the three of us, he was the youngest. It pained me, as it did everyone, that he had already gone through so much at such a young age. No one in our family, myself included, understood how it felt to have lost both parents in the way he did. None of us could imagine the courage now needed to testify against one and defend the other. But, like all of us, Caleb was doing this out of the love we shared for our mother and the justice we hoped it would serve her memory. That was all the motivation any one of us needed.

He left the doorway following the woman downstairs, about to take the stand in the next few minutes.

It was an entirely chaotic time. There was so much confusion. First, I was informed I could not, under any circumstances, be present in the court room if Caleb or anyone else was testifying. Then, I was told it was perfectly fine to sit in on his testimony just as long as I had already provided mine. I didn't know what to do, so I went with the option I favored.

I followed family downstairs to the courtroom and shuffled in behind them as we took our seats in the wooden rows. Before I could even sit down, the judge pointed me out.

"Is that Monica?" he spotted me from his chair. All eyes turned around.

"Yes, Judge. We saw to it that …" Jennifer replied, but the judge waved his hand and didn't seem to be listening to her.

"No. No. Get her out of here," he said.

Immediately, I turned around and was escorted out of the court room. I sat alone outside the transparent, glass doors on a black marble bench in the busy, bright white hallway lined with court room doors. I waited eagerly to see Caleb take the stand. If I couldn't hear, I wanted to at least see what was happening. Caleb was nervous, so I thought it might help calm his nerves if he could see my support from the hall.

When I saw him approach and take the stand next to the judge, I stood up. Caleb was an entertainer at heart and I had never seen him so serious. I stood at the door, trying to be in his line of sight. What I didn't notice was the secretary from upstairs who had become very familiar with my face and our case. She turned around in her seat. She must have seen me staring in and pacing the hallway because she slowly got up to remove herself and came to the hallway, steaming in frustration.

"What are you doing! You can't be out here!" she yelled.

"Jennifer said I could wait outside," I said confused and desperately eager to stay where I was. *Please don't move me!*

"No, no, no, no, no. She must not be thinking clearly! She has a lot on her plate today. If they see you out here it could ruin the whole thing! We don't want this to be a mistrial! You guys have waited too long for that. No, sweetie, you need to go upstairs." She then walked me back to the upstairs library.

Irritated as I entered in the empty library, I sat back down in my uncomfortable, stiff skirt that I desperately wanted to exchange for sweatpants and placed my head in my hands. It was finally our day in court, and I had given my testimony. But it seemed that no matter how long I had waited, and cried, and stressed, and dreamed of this day, I was only going to be a tiny piece of it. Someone had failed to tell me that after years of jerking my emotions around, I wasn't going to be able to hear or see any of it! *Breathe, breathe.* This was about Mom! Had I come all this way just to sit and wait alone while family and friends sat in the courtroom hearing every detail? Was this going to be a day I would hear about from everyone else for the rest of my life?

Even Ian was allowed to take a seat in the middle of the room in a large, comfy chair. *Ugh!* I was revolted at the whole miserable irony.

Searching within myself, I knew that all I truly wanted was for Ian to be sentenced and found guilty. My own feelings would have to stay on the sidelines. I would just have to keep wading in the water until verdict day.

Time passed faster as I made small talk with Mom's divorce lawyer. She was a Hispanic woman, sweet and kind-hearted, and another person who was aware of Mom's dangerous relationship. She told me that Ian had discovered our address in the apartments, because she had accidentally sent the divorce paperwork to Ian with Mom's new address on it.

During our small talk, I learned there had been many people close to Mom, her friends, family and even Evan, who tried to help, too. She told me about how they had tried to persuade her and warn her about the dangers she would be stepping into even long before I started to. One of Mom's best friends from the hospital, Kristie, later told me that while Mom sat in the moving truck with Ian, Evan was texting her and desperately trying to talk her out of her decision.

My family flooded back into the library over an hour later. I jolted up, trying to analyze their expressions. Caleb was quiet. He plopped himself right back into his seat and stared at the table with one hand on his forehead and his foot twitching.

"What happened?" I asked, desperately craving an answer.

"I messed it up."

"What?!" I looked over at Junior. "Junior, what happened?"

I knew Caleb would be too hard on himself. He was under more pressure than any of us. His father was here in court, while mine was sitting in the front row. I couldn't even begin to imagine what he was feeling.

The family revealed to me that the same lawyer who questioned me and desperately tried to make me look like a fool was ruthless towards Caleb. They told me he badgered Caleb to the point of professional concern, throwing out random topics that seemed to have no relevance like, "Did you have a dog?"

My family said they waited for the judge to intervene as the lawyer appeared completely out of line, but nothing happened. From their stories, it seemed that the grimy lawyer was seeking to break Caleb's spirit by throwing him off and pricking at his emotionally damaged relationship with his father. For Ian's defense, Caleb seemed to be an easy target and their best chance to rile up and discredit us.

Caleb was hard on himself which made me even angrier for not being able to sit in the court room to hear it for myself. Although my family told me what they could remember, I knew they would leave out details because during family parties, they had never been very good at retelling stories.

By lunchtime, all of us had spent the entire morning boiling in a pot of nerves and were told to break for an hour lunch. Junior, Caleb and I rested at a McDonald's nearby. Our thoughts were spiraling as we went over every response to the questions that morning. We persistently asked ourselves: *Was it all enough? Would our words be enough for the jury?* There were still so much we wanted to know. All the experts in the case still needed to testify, and there was no way to know how this would end.

When we returned from lunch, Carlita was the last person from our family waiting to testify. She was Mom's youngest sister and an honest-to-the-core kind of woman. She was blunt and powerful, and her greatest weapon was her sense of humor. That, and her unforeseen ability to kick anyone's ass. She was always the fun that came to every family gathering. She could have even the hardest of souls laughing for hours. However, her laughter was in short supply in that moment. It was strange for me to see her joyful, witty attitude become so scared and shaken as she waited for her turn on the stand.

When they called her downstairs, she walked in a fear greater than anyone else's. She had despised Ian for years and had a history with him long before I knew who he was. At her house, Ian was never welcomed, never allowed to be present for family gatherings, parties or holidays. For years, even before Mom was gone, she and Ian despised each other and never spoke. Today, she had to stand before him.

Days prior to that fateful Sunday, Carlita and Mom discussed leaving Ian. Mom had disclosed to her that she would be taking the money out of their account and leaving him for good. It was also during that time that Mom confided in her with a dangerous statement, "If I go missing, you know who did it." Mom went on to tell Carlita that she and Evan had a home they were looking at.

Tia Carlita urged Mom to come stay with her. "Why wait?" she had told her, trying to make her leave at that very moment, but Mom, as strong, joyous and independent as she was, refused her invitation.

I waited upstairs while Tia Carlita gave her testimony. Upon her return, she sighed with the same great relief I had.

"How did it go?" we all asked curiously.

With her humor coming back she replied, "Ugh, I didn't even want to look at him. I didn't even want his eyes on me. I just scooted back behind the judge's seat and there's a spot where it blocks his face, so I just stayed there. I just answered the questions and got the hell out of there."

Everyone from the family had given their testimony. It was only the first day and it strangely felt longer than the years we had waited for it to come. As we left the court house, we knew we were all in for a long, sleepless week.

...

The next morning, as the blue daylight slowly crept through the windows, I lay on my air mattress imagining what the day would bring. After my niece and nephew left for daycare, the house atmosphere returned to a peaceful silence. Junior, Caleb, and I gathered our attention to the day ahead. We dressed in our nicest attire, bundled up in our coats, and headed out into the gloomy winter air.

My heightened anxiety returned each day that I sat in the same stiff, wooden benches. When court began, the judge allowed Caleb and me to be present during the rest of the trial. After exchanging greetings and words of encouragement with everyone, I noticed a familiar face in the last row behind me. It was Evan. He sat there with worry on his face and had come along with his new wife. I hadn't seen nor heard from him since the day he asked me to let him be.

As much as it pained me to see him sitting with the beautiful, bright blonde who was now his wife, I knew that he, too, had been healing over the last few years. Not for a second could I blame him. But that didn't stop my heart from aching at the sight of the woman on his arm and the absence of Mom next to him.

During court, I carefully listened to the experts' testimonies and began to understand why it had taken so many years for this day to come. I had no idea there were several people whose time needed to be coordinated and synced for this trial on this day: the bank manager, the cell phone tower experts, a Sprint phone service expert, a US Cellular phone service expert, a Trans union expert, and most disturbing of all, the coroner and the medical examiner.

Each person was crucial and essential for explaining details of the case. Nearly each and every one of them had a testimony supported by years of education, experience, and data. They all made some meticulous, in-depth presentations that would allow the jury to see the details of that Sunday.

Part of Jennifer's job was to point out to the jury how all of that evidence was tied to Ian and presented his motive for committing such a selfish monstrosity. I realized court is not a carefree kind of gal. She demands order and is strict with a capital S. Every single detail had to be thoroughly discussed, explained, and cross examined by the defense. There was no room for error and there couldn't be any reason why a member of the jury should be confused about a single thing. The entire sequence of events had to be air tight, because the entire case depended on the evidence. After each expert provided their testimony and was cross examined by the defense, our hearts were all asking, *Is it enough?* The next four days of questions and answers came to this conclusion:

Mom and Ian shared an account where his mother's money was kept. The Bank of America expert explained the statements each month, over several months, recorded increments of one hundred to two hundred dollars being withdrawn consistently every week. Both Ian and Mom had debit cards to this account and the expert explained which card had completed which transactions. A receipt from Mom's purse matched the number to the card she had in her wallet, showing she was the owner of a certain number, leaving Ian the owner of the other. We knew who was making which transactions, and Mom was taking the money out slowly. Just days before Sunday, Mom had withdrawn a large final sum of four thousand dollars, leaving Ian with nearly nothing.

After Mom dropped me off at Jim's house, she and Caleb returned home. Caleb asked Mom if he could go to his friend's house, and she agreed. She took him there about 5:00 PM, and when she returned home, she was presumed to be alone. They proved she was scheduled for work that night, just as she had been almost every night.

Before her routine nap, records show that she made some calls to her sister Carlita and to Junior. The detectives proved that while Mom was at home, a car identical to Ian's was caught on the security camera at the Bank of America drive-thru. The bank was forty minutes away on the other side of town. The footage shows the car pulled up to the ATM, and records from the statements show the balance was checked at that exact same time which was in the amount of two hundred dollars.

Detectives believe this is when Ian discovered that almost nothing remained in the account. With no one other than Mom to blame, Ian drove straight home. Detectives tested the drive themselves in their own cars, and their times proved Ian didn't have time to stop anywhere else.

When Ian arrived home, something happened that no one other than Ian and Mom will ever know. The truth exists only in the depth of Ian's memory. He may have known he had lost all control of Mom, and he was going to lose her again. He may have known she was leaving him, and he knew she had the money to do so. Somehow, Mom was forced into the trunk of her own car and then shot several times. She remained there as Ian drove out of the garage.

Detectives believe Ian drove around town trying to find a place to leave the car. First, he parked her Pontiac on a quiet neighborhood street less than 10 minutes away. This is where our witness saw a tall Hispanic man staring into the trunk of a bright white car. But with the likelihood of being seen, they believe Ian eventually relocated the car in front of Caleb's friend's house whom he was visiting at that moment. From there, Ian left and walked all the way back home.

During his walk home, one of Caleb's calls made a world of difference. His attempt caught a local cell phone tower and 'pinged' off it. The cell phone tower expert provided the explanation that Ian was in the general location just blocks away from Mom's car that night.

When Ian returned home, he was met with Caleb standing firmly inside the locked door asking him the first question we needed to know, "Where's Mom?" And here, my story began.

Our attorneys were convinced Ian intended for people to find Mom and conclude that something must have happened to her after she dropped Caleb off; that she was possibly mugged or robbed; nothing Ian could be blamed for.

When police found her car, investigators analyzed the entire vehicle. The detectives said they found the driver's seat placed all the way back, comfortable for someone of six feet. I had driven Mom's car and had never had to move the seat back because she was as short as I was, barely five feet tall.

As I listened intently to the prosecution and the defense take turns questioning the experts, I noticed that the only defense Ian's lawyers could summon was "It wasn't him" and "How do we know it wasn't anyone else?" There didn't seem to be any other argument they were willing to entertain. I was especially thankful they did not, at any point in trial, argue he could not possibly be guilty because he truly loved Mom and therefore could never commit such an act. If they had dared step into that realm of lies, I may have flown over the banister or choked on my own gasping breath. Strangely enough, somewhere in my heart, I don't even believe his lawyers saw him as an innocent man.

Ian's lawyers were right about one thing. There was no evidence that linked Ian directly to the crime. Our evidence was circumstantial, meaning it was only the circumstances that alluded to Ian's motive which made me sink in fear since

I understood just how careful and capable Ian could truly be. There were no prints, no DNA, no weapon and no close-up camera footage anywhere during his half mile walk that captured his face. Ian's defense used this lack of evidence to their advantage and argued that he was simply out for a casual walk that night, gathering some fresh air. They argued that the cell tower ping did not show a precise location, only a general location.

"This isn't evidence!" they rebutted. "Hundreds of other people were in that general location at that time, too. I could have been in that location! You could have been in that location!" Ian's lawyers saw the evidence as laughable and nothing that even came close to conclude he was a guilty man.

Yet, while our attorneys argued that all the circumstances pointed to no one other than Ian, he strangely kept his composure. It wasn't until halfway through the trial, after many of the experts had provided their testimonies, that I saw a glimpse of Ian's nerves. His hands were shaking as he brought a pen to the paper in front of him, trying to communicate silently with his lawyer.

In the entire time, it was the only moment he showed any indication he might be nervous. He was always as solid as a stone, yet as hollow as a paper cup. He was the type of person who has unrealistic confidence and the belief he has every ounce of control. But no matter how he saw it, it was not in his control.

His barren eyes were still just as impossible to read. He sat quietly and remained still. His hands were folded on his lap, and his glasses rested on his nose as he glared at the jury, leaning back in his leather chair. He looked neither nervous nor timid; neither confident nor assured. If he felt anything at all, he masked it well.

During the entire week listening to grueling, sickening details about Mom's death and how she died, Ian shed not a single tear. As for the rest of us, we sat with tissue boxes in every row, in every hand and at every eye.

Every so often, as the medical examiner spoke, Ian would carefully glance over his shoulder at the dozens of us sitting behind him. Everyone was always prepared to strike him with the sternest face if he dared to lay his eyes on us.

On the last day of court, I awoke early, vividly aware that today, we might finally have an answer. Every piece of evidence had been presented to the jury and Ian had a choice to make. He could either stand before the jury and allow our lawyers, as well as his own, to question him on the stand. Or, he could choose to let everything speak for itself and not say a word on his own behalf.

If he chose to stand before us, our attorneys were prepared to ask him questions I desperately wanted them to. However, to no one's surprise, he chose to remain silent. Jennifer believed if he took that risk, he could easily incriminate himself and destroy any chance he had of being found innocent. Although the judge methodically explained to the jury that Ian's choice to refuse the stand should not be held against him, I know it had an effect on them. I also knew that if the jury had the opportunity to see my entire life flash up on a screen, or any one of our lives with Ian for that matter, they would feel the same truth we all felt.

Regrettably, the justice system would not allow us to discuss any other history than what was agreed upon; no matter how much it would illuminate Ian's guilt. No matter how much the details of our lives would paint the Picasso of pictures the jury needed, the lawyers all had to stick to the agreed upon topics. So, as the judge briefed the jury on their obligation to come to a unanimous decision, not tainted with any bias, I prayed everything explained over the last five days was enough for them see the truth.

"All rise for the jury," a guard shouted.

In the front row, I stood with Caleb by my side. I squeezed his hand on the banister and watched as the twelve jury members were dismissed. When the very last one left, I turned around to see everyone's eager faces simply drop. The next time we saw the jury, they would have reached a verdict that could forever change our lives.

...

Swinging in Uncertainty

COURT HAD TAKEN ALL MY FEELINGS captive and held me in a tsunami type of emotional prison. Every fiber within me felt as if I were being crushed by thousands of pounds. Every single molecule my body produced was working to keep me sane since time was now the only thing standing between us and a verdict. After several years of waiting, believing this day would never come and enduring the torment of Ian, I now sat at the long gray table in the upstairs waiting area with my family. Mom's fate swung in the hands of twelve people who had never even met her.

The wait brought unfathomable amounts of pain to my soul. The anxiety was so high, so intense, so agonizing that I could have easily sprinted ten miles and still had energy to spare. I dangled on the edge of my seat as my thoughts raced, evaporating into newer, wilder thoughts. I squeezed Mom's bracelet around my wrist in an attempt to summon enough strength to calm myself and wait.

We gathered in the conference room near the hall of offices for lunch. Caleb, Junior and Dad were all huddled near me as we tried to enjoy the food that had been ordered for us. Pizza, usually a food I could consume by the pound, was sitting on my plate getting cold. I had no appetite and hadn't eaten a thing all day. My family filled in the seats around me and began to serve themselves. They all tried to create a conversation outside the pressing topic.

"I tell you what. If he's not found guilty, I'm jumping over that bench and going ham on his ass," Junior said. He sat across from me, with no food in front of him. He was trying to devise a plan of attack he believed he could get away with.

I smiled, "You know the guards will probably put you in jail if you do that; and not to mention, you have two kids."

"So? So, I spend one night in jail. It would be worth it. That would be just fine." He was completely serious, and I knew it.

Dad did too, because he shook his head in the same way we all did when Junior said something crazy. I looked at Dad who was sitting in the chair next to me with nothing on his plate either. When the waiting became too uncomfortable, he'd stand up and take a walk around the offices to loosen the tension. He also began to look for Junior, who had left a while ago.

Trying to distract myself from the news we were all waiting to hear, I chimed in on the family conversation. Everyone had finished their plates, but the talking was pointless. Within seconds, we were all brought back to the anticipation of the verdict. We were not able to block it out of our minds.

"What if he's found not guilty?" someone asked.

The question was real, and it terrified me. I grabbed my phone to ignore the chatter and saw through the corner of my eye a blue flashing light, which meant I had a message. There was a text from Jennifer sent just minutes ago, "They've reached a verdict. Come downstairs."

Slowly, I looked up as my family was chatting away.

"What is it?" Caleb asked. He saw the terrified look on my face.

"They've reached a verdict," I managed to mumble.

"They've reached a verdict?" he exclaimed loud enough to grab everyone's attention.

"They reached a verdict?" my cousin repeated. Everyone turned their head toward me.

"Yeah," I responded. "Jennifer just texted me. They've reached a verdict. We need to go downstairs."

Instantly, everyone leapt from their seats and scattered to clean up the open boxes of salads and chicken wings spread across the table. We all rushed downstairs. I quickly texted all Mom's friends who had gone elsewhere for lunch and urged them to *"Come back now! They've reached a verdict!"*

"I can't believe they reached a decision so fast!" my tia said as we all bypassed the elevator and darted down the dark, spiraling stairwell.

"I know! My God, that's crazy!" my cousin replied.

It had only been a little over an hour since the jury began their deliberation. We all jogged down the steps as quickly as possible and busted open the exit doors, unleashing the dozens of us into the bright lobby. I looked at Caleb as we raced side by side, catching our breath. Our eyes spoke hope in the somber silence.

Junior was up ahead, leading all of us. I glanced behind me to see my tias, tios, cousins and family friends running along with us.

When we arrived at the courtroom doors, we halted and looked inside, making sure we were able to enter. Jennifer saw us crowded at the door and came to meet us.

"They've reached a verdict?" we shouted as she stepped out.

"Yes." Her smile was calm.

"Is that a good sign?" someone asked.

"It could be. The judge is going to announce the verdict after…" Unable to focus on anything other than the swinging of my fragile heart, I withdrew. My mind sprinted down the infinite number of outcomes that lay in the seconds ahead.

"You okay?" Jennifer asked as she brushed my shoulder.

"Uh, not really," I answered. I must have looked as frail as I felt. I wanted to know one thing and one thing only: *What's the verdict?*

She smiled, "We'll bring you guys in, in just a couple of minutes."

"Okay, thank you," we all said as she stepped back inside.

"Hey, you guys, let's pray before we go in," my cousin said, catching everyone's attention. Everyone nodded in agreement, "Yeah, let's pray for Titi Irma." We slowly gathered into a large circle and latched our palms tightly together in the busy hall to pray for the news we were about to receive.

We stood unified. The connection was flowing through each hand as we bowed our heads and were led in prayer by one of the men in our family. As his words began, so did my tears. I opened my eyes as they hit the floor. I clenched both my cousin's and Caleb's hands, begging for the Great Lord Almighty, Jesus Christ, to give us justice in these next few moments. I also begged that if we didn't, that he would take care of me no matter the outcome.

Looking up after our solemn "Amen", my cousin saw my drenched face and brought me close.

Before we swarmed inside, Jennifer came outside to inform us that when the verdict was announced, we were not allowed to show any emotion that might draw attention. We couldn't shout, scream, or be overly hysterical in any way that would cause a scene or distract from the trial. Nothing could interfere with the process. So, instead of releasing all the chaotic, wild flying emotions that each of us was battling hard to keep under the radar, we also had to find the strength to keep it all together after the verdict was spoken.

"If you feel like that's too much, just put your head down, or quietly excuse yourself," Jennifer explained.

I wasn't going anywhere. I had waited eight years for this day. I had to keep my instinctive desire to release my emotions together somehow, no matter what the verdict was.

If that was going to happen, I had to get as much of it out now as I could. So, I stood in my cousin's arms, trying to drown out all my tears.

A few minutes after Jennifer's briefing, the guard came out to open the door. We all immediately rushed in.

Junior darted into the front row and sat at the very front end, closest to where Ian would be. I sat next to him, and Caleb came to my other side. I turned around to see everyone finding their place in the rows behind me. All of our loving support continued to flood into the seats for the next several minutes until eventually every seat on Mom's side was filled with flushed eyes, hopeful smiles and worried hearts.

With every seat soon taken on Mom's side, some unwillingly situated themselves in the back rows of Ian's side. As our squad of support continued flooding into the court room, I noticed one of Ian's lawyers was turned around in his chair. He was taken aback as he stared at the vast sea of loving faces. His eyes appeared soft as he quietly gasped at the sight.

"Wow," he whispered to himself.

As I continued to gaze around the room, I noticed an increase in the amount of guards standing in every corner. They appeared to swarm the entire room. I assumed it was protocol to bring in more heat during a verdict because people like Junior had crazy plans.

"You see all the guards in here?" I whispered to Junior.

His eyes widened. "Ya know man!" he laughed. "Like for real!"

"Yeah, because people like you want to jump the guard rail! They're not stupid," I pointed out.

Dad, realizing Junior was sitting so close, got up from his seat and came in between us.

"Here, sweetie, scoot down," he said. He realized Junior was nowhere near joking in his earlier remarks.

As the shuffling of papers and the opening and closing of doors started to quiet, so did our soft chatter.

"All rise for the jury."

We stood. I placed one hand on the banister and grabbed Caleb's hand with the other as we waited for the jury to trail in and take their seats. As each person appeared, one by one sitting before us, I frantically looked upon them, desperate to read an answer written on their faces.

"You may be seated."

A tall, thin man professionally dressed in the seat next to the judge stood to read us Mom's deeply longed for answer; every one of our hearts stalled in uncertainty. He spoke: "We the people of the State of Illinois find the defendant in the charge of first-degree murder, guilty; in the charge of concealment of a homicide, we find the defendant, guilty."

Carefully restored with rapidly, blossoming peace, my spirit sang. When the words guilty were released into the air, the heart of every friend, sister, son and lost lover felt the peace that had been finally returned to Mom's life.

Ian threw himself back into his chair and nearly fell right out of it. Steaming with anger, he shook his head and with trembling hands, nervously brushing his withered mustache.

"Members of the jury, the State of Illinois thanks you for your service," he said.

For the longest minutes that it took for the jury to be dismissed, deep, crippling cries sparked quietly within us. Voices trembled. I kept my face down, for if I looked up, I would have erupted. I could hear the rapidly flowing tears rushing from everyone, and I knew everyone was fighting to hold them back. For a few seconds longer, my strong desire to flood the earth with my thankful cries was held inside. But then, when the jury left, I released everything. My knees gave out from under me, and the sound of blissful cries immersed the room.

I looked up at Caleb's brown eyes. They were illuminated in a way I had never seen. This precious moment had given them a special glow. He gasped with a perfect balance of shock and relief.

Fiercely reprieved, we latched our arms around one another; tears cascaded down our faces. Over Caleb's shoulder, I saw Junior in Dad's arms. When he let Dad go, he threw his arms around me and held me close with the most tranquil smile I'd ever seen on his face. He wasn't crying. He was at peace. And he had an expression that seemed to have released all his anger from the uncertainty and injustice experienced during all these years. He rocked me side to side as I screamed my cries out onto his chest, and with a calm voice whispered to me the very words I was thinking, "It's over, Sis. It's over."

In between my gasping of tears, I sobbed, "I know, I know."

In the past, Ian always returned; somehow, some way. To hear those words aloud now with the truth they had just been given, felt as if the chains to my past had been broken. At last, I was free from Ian's grasp. The truth was real, and it was final; Ian was no longer a part of our lives and never would he be again.

The guards took Ian back into the holding cells as our glistening smiles were joyously overwhelmed with justice. I didn't even see him leave for the news had overtaken me. Everyone rejoiced with passionate hugs, kisses and sparkling eyes that came from both happiness and sadness.

The courtroom staff dispersed long before any of us took notice. After some time, Jennifer kindly suggested we move out into the hall so that the guards could lock up the courtroom.

Our beaming happiness and rivers of tears continued in the hallway. I made sure to wrap my arms around every single person who showed their support for Mom's memory: her friends, coworkers, and Evan. But most of all to our powerful, astounding team of lawyers, who spent hours over the years to give Mom this final victory. In the blissful chaos, I spotted

Jennifer and our attorneys and immediately rushed to them, thanking them with appreciation for everything they had done to bring our family to this moment. It was because of them that I was here smiling. Because of them I had been released from Ian's clutches, and Mom's spirit was finally able to rest in peaceful freedom. I hugged each of them repeating, "Thank you, thank you so much."

It is within every piece of my heart that I admire and love each of them. Never will I be able to repay them for their efforts that have forever changed the way I look at my past and the way I will look at my future.

"It feels like closing the doors to an evil past. His reign of terror in our life is finally over," were the words I told the *Chicago Tribune* reporter when he questioned me. When the reporter started interviewing Caleb and Junior, I drifted away to continue sharing the radiating glory with everyone.

Friends and family began to disperse and leave us with loving goodbyes. A small group of us, still soaking up the beautiful news, now stood outside the courtroom doors that we had been coming to for the past eight years.

I could still remember how I sat upstairs during a large conference meeting with everyone involved in this case. We were then told that, on a scale of one to ten, our chances of taking this to trial was only one or two. At that time, my hopes had been destroyed, thinking Ian would get away with all of his monstrosities, and that Mom would have left this world without any peace. But now, to be here with a guilty verdict said we were a ten all along.

"He'll be moved in a couple days to the state prison and from there he's not looking at any chance of probation," Jennifer's words pleased every ear.

"Thank God," my Tia Carlita whispered.

"Yeah, he's never getting out." Jennifer smiled.

I thanked them repeatedly, and my heart was spilling over in appreciation.

We exchanged our last goodbyes. "If you need anything, you let us know," Jennifer said.

They provided me a form to complete if I wanted to be notified of anything that happened to Ian during his imprisonment. I stuffed it in my pocket, reluctant to have anything else to do with him, but instead kindly replied, "I'll think about it, thank you."

Detective Bleecher approached, "Monica, you have a friend in me for life." His words were warm and genuine and his hug tight. I could only be thankful that fate had chosen him to be the detective for Mom's case. He was one individual who cared so deeply that he came to feel just like family.

After every goodbye was said, every hug was exchanged and every tear was dried, Junior, Caleb and I made our way to the tall, cathedral glass doors of the court house. I buttoned up my coat, tucked in my scarf and put on my gloves, bracing myself for the harsh winter air. I walked, staring at the ground, the verdict still making me feel as if I was gliding on a cloud of another world, another planet that had never been this kind to me. When I stepped outside there was no wind, no chill, and no coldness. The sky was the warmest blue, and the sun was radiant.

...

Epilogue: Sentencing

"**Good Afternoon, your Honor.** My name is Monica Medina, I'm the daughter of our beloved mother, Irma Arroyo. To stand before you today is a dream; it doesn't feel real and it may not for a long time. To stand before you today means something of truly great significance in my life. It is a day so significant that no words come close to capturing its importance. Nonetheless, it's a day that we've been waiting for for far too long.

I never imagined we would ever make it to this point; to imagine it felt like wishful thinking. But now, to finally be here is simply beyond feelings that words could express. I stand here, knowing that the terror and fear I have lived my whole life since I was a young child is finally over. Knowing that the horrible life I have lived and endured is finally at its end and will no longer keep me in its grasp. I feel I can finally break free from an evil past.

Though my heart is happy for this day of justice, we've made it here without our mother. When she passed, I lost a huge part of my life. I know that for as long as I live, I will never be whole again. I will forever miss a love that I once had. As a result of this senseless evil, I have lost the opportunity for many memories. Though for years I have cried immense amounts of tears and experienced much pain, I have finally come to a point where I hold no hate in my heart. There is no hate towards this spineless person sitting here with us today, and that is because I know that he was not lucky enough to experience a life with the same person I did; that we all did. I know that when she was with us, we were fortunate enough to have enjoyed the best of her, and the true and honest person she was. We experienced time with her when she was truly able to be herself. With us she was able to take all her guards down and experience the joy and freedom that life offers. We were able to spend time with her when she could think and speak freely, relax and enjoy herself, having peace for a moment of time. We were blessed to have felt special, protected, and greatly loved by her.

When I say that I miss everything about her, I do mean everything. I have fond memories of her hysterical laugh, her warm hugs, and her kind voice. Facing the last eight years without her has been indescribably difficult and will always continue to be. In the beginning, I faced some major depression, lacking care for many things and people. I soon told myself that I would do everything in my power to experience every joy life has to offer; that he would not break my spirit. I would embrace life, treat others with kindness as she did, and cherish those close to me with every ounce of love in my heart. I understand all too well how suddenly life can slip away. There is nothing I could ever say, no words that will ever measure up to provide the picture you need to understand the bond we had, nor the amazing person she was. No words even exist to describe the suffering and terror that we endured together. On this day, we have been relieved from this past, and I know she is finally free."

Ian's eyes firmly focused upon me as I read my statement aloud, the judge and my family listening. It was the first chance I'd been given to speak to him and tell him how I felt since leaving the house that Sunday. The moment allowed me to lay my heart open and have his ears hear my years of pain since the day he had taken Mom away from me. Looking out at them all, I stood paralyzed, nervous to speak. But as I stood closer to him, I noticed something had changed. His presence was different.

All my life, I distinctly recall looking at this man, knowing him and fearing him. I came to know his voice, his expressions and his triggers all too well. But, looking at him now, I realized that I no longer knew him at all. The passing years had deteriorated a connection that was once all I knew and now, it was as if he was a complete stranger. I almost questioned why I was reading these words to him in the first place.

Regardless of my impression, it was him. He didn't look it or voice it, but underneath the aging body it was the same man that had brought me those years of ruined memories. It was the same man who had taken Mom, and I was no longer afraid of him.

My fear of Ian was replaced by pity. I saw him as a gravely sad man. He was one who was never able to change or find his own happiness, and he kept others from finding it. He was a man who, in his fifty years of living, never figured it out. And now, he would never get the chance to, for the judge placed his sentencing at sixty-five years to life in prison.

After receiving our guilty verdict, I was ignited to celebrate. Mom's presence was in the air, and I felt her memory deserved honor. Everyone had gone home, but I couldn't let the day end without something more. I called my oldest cousin after getting back to Junior's house and told her I wanted all of us to go out and celebrate.

"Yeah, I agree," she said. "I think that's a good idea."

I searched the internet and called a bunch of restaurants, but had no luck when they asked, "How many are in your party?"

"Let's see, um, twenty-five," I answered. I tried sounding casual, but none of the places seemed to have any availability. I tried to think: *Where to go, where to go, where to go?* When suddenly, I was reminded of the restaurant my boyfriend and I had gone to on our first date. I called the place.

"Hi, I'm wondering if you have any availability to seat a party of twenty-five. I know it's late, but…" I glanced at the time, it was 6:00 PM, later than I thought.

"Give me a minute, let me check and see," the host replied.

I kept my hope strong: *Please have space, please have space.*

"Hello?" she came back to the phone.

"Yes!"

"Okay, yeah we can seat you."

"Really?" I shouted, surprised.

Two hours later, for the first time since Mom had passed, the entire family was gathered together. We took the time to relax from the week we'd had and caught up on everyone's lives. Many of us, including myself, had flown in from out of state, so I knew how rare it was to have everyone surrounding the dinner table at the same time.

After I finished my meal, I went to the bar and asked them for their cheapest champagne. I wanted to celebrate, but I also wasn't made out of money. The bartender pointed to their cheaper selection on the menu and assured me two bottles would be enough to serve at least eighteen adults. I gave her my debit card, signed my receipt, and returned to my seat at the long table of laughing faces that brought such warmth to my heart.

I continued catching up with my cousin and meeting her newborn when two waiters came in with four trays of tall champagne glasses. As they set the trays down and began pouring each glass, everyone looked around the room asking, "What's this?" Their confused faces made me laugh.

"I didn't order this, did you?" they continued, "Where did this come from?" But the waiters said nothing and continued to pass around the glasses.

"What are we celebrating?" asked one of lively servers.

Everyone looked at one another, stumped by what we should say.

My Tia Carlita broke the silence with her glass raised, "A guilty verdict."

Irma Rosa Arroyo
June 9, 1964 – May 31, 2009
Forever in Our Hearts & Memories

CPSIA information can be obtained
at www.ICGtesting.com
Printed in the USA
BVHW041413230323
660889BV00005B/31

9 781950 906680